SECRET ORDER

Bob Clyman

BROADWAY PLAY PUBLISHING INC
224 E 62nd St, NY, NY 10065
www.broadwayplaypub.com
ifno@broadwayplaypub.com

SECRET ORDER
© Copyright 2014 by Bob Clyman

Cover art by Doug Katz, JamArtz.com

First printing: February 2014
Second printing: November 2015

I S B N: 978-0-88145-574-8

Book design: Marie Donovan
Word processing: Microsoft Word
Typographic controls: Xerox Ventura Publisher 2.0 P E
Typeface: Palatino
Printed and bound in the U S A

SECRET ORDER was commissioned by the Ensemble
Studio Theatre/Alfred P Sloan Foundation Science &
Technology Project and received its world premiere at
the Ensemble Studio Theatre in New York on 8 April
2002. The cast and creative contributors were:

WILLIAM SHUMWAY	Liam Craig
ROBERT BROCK	James Murtaugh
ALICE CURITON	Amy Love
SAUL ROTH	Joel Rooks
Director	Jamie Richards
Set	Bruce Goodrich
Lighting	Michael Lincoln
Costumes	Amela Baksic
Sound	Robert Gould
Stage manager	Timothy Gallagher

SECRET ORDER was produced Off-Broadway by Merrimack Repertory Theatre and received its opening at 59E59 Theatres (Theatre A) in New Ypork on 9 November 2007. The cast and creative contributors were:

WILLIAM SHUMWAY .... Dan Colman
ROBERT BROCK .... Larry Pine
ALICE CURITON .... Jessi Campbell
SAUL ROTH .... Kenneth Tigar

Director .... Charles Towers
Set .... Bill Clarke
Lighting .... Dan Kotlowitz
Costumes .... Martha Hally
Sound .... James Whoolery
Stage manager .... Jon William Goldman

CHARACTERS

WILLIAM SHUMWAY, *early 30s. Immunologist. A passionately curious scientist in cancer research and rising star at the Hill-Matheson Institute. By nature, gentle and isolated.*

ROBERT BROCK, *50s. Immunologist and Director of Hill-Matheson. SHUMWAY's mentor, a charismatic man of great intelligence and ambition. More awkward in his personal life but capable of a gruff kind of affection.*

ALICE CURITON, *21. A student in SHUMWAY's lab. A bright, "mouthy" spitfire, indifferent to etiquette.*

SAUL ROTH, *67. Chief of Toxicology at Hill-Matheson. Plays at being the amiable philosopher but is in fact a very political animal. BROCK's rival for power.*

Two acts. Running time: 2 hours with intermission

NOTE

The use of back slash (/) marks towards the end of a line signifies where the next character speaking should interrupt.

If a back slash precedes an ellipsis (/...) at the end of a line, the interruption should come in as quickly as possible after the last word but not interrupt it.

If a line ends with an ellipsis but no back slash, the lack of a full stop suggests that the character is implicitly pointing toward some completion of his thought. In many of those instances in the character might have asked something to the effect of, "Do you know what I mean", if he had completed the sentence.

If an ellipsis takes place within a speech rather than at the end of it, it means the character has interrupted himself to pursue a different thought.

ACT ONE

(*Lights up on* WILLIAM SHUMWAY, *a cell biologist in his early thirties from the University of Illinois, as he walks on stage.*)

SHUMWAY: (*Tapping the microphone, looking into the wing*) Is this on? (*Turning to the audience*) Hello. My name is Doctor William Shumway. On behalf of the program committee, welcome to the university's Monday lecture series. Afterwards, there'll be something to eat. For those of you who came to today's symposium expecting to hear Doctor Vregel in Flemish Studies read from his new collection of poems, he was suddenly called out of town, and the program committee has asked me to fill in. I'm a cell biologist here at Illinois, my area's cancer research, so, if there's any logic to the process, I have to assume I wasn't their first choice. Ordinarily, I would've tried like the dickens to get out of it. I don't really like talking in front of groups or being in groups or talking, but this morning, the most amazing thing…then suddenly, complete coincidence, I was being asked to speak. (*Beat*) So, imagine your body's a community, and your cells are the people who live there. The dream of every cell is to be immortal…to make endless copies of itself, but the community can only use so many liver cells and no more than two eyes, so your cells need to cooperate…send signals to each other…"yes, it's your turn to divide" or "no, please wait in line."

Actually, it's a lot like this town meeting I went to, where everyone had an opinion, they're all talking at once, but what makes this really confusing is you've got ten billion cells, so the meeting feels more like China with no one in charge. But it all works out in the end…everyone gives a little, gets a little, because that's what a community is. *(Slight beat)* Except every now and then, you get a bad apple…the kind of cell that just won't listen to "no". He never used to be a problem, but then he mutated into a cancer cell…pumping out copies, who also keep pumping out copies…a virtual riot of malignant, unstoppable vanity, until the day comes you notice they've driven out all of the decent folk and taken over the town. Everything we've tried… surgery, chemo…comes at a terrible cost. So it occurred to me, what if instead of attacking the cancer directly, I could turn it against itself. This was three years ago, and you can't imagine how difficult technically, but I just finished running a set of experiments, and… now remember, everything I've done so far has been just in a Petri dish, nothing on actual mice, let alone… and again it's only one set of experiments, so this is completely premature, but I think I may have figured out how to cure cancer. *(Beat)* How am I doing on time?

(SHUMWAY's *phone rings. Lights up on* DR ROBERT BROCK, *phone in hand, Director of Cancer Research at the Hill-Matheson Institute.* SHUMWAY *answers his cell phone)*

SHUMWAY: Hello?

BROCK: Listen, I just read your paper, grab a pen. In your letter… "Do I think you should try to publish in *Cell*?" Four days in a Petri dish? Don't waste the stamps. Maybe in *Immunology* or *Trends*, I don't know where you got the idea it's ready for *Cell*.

SHUMWAY: I'm sorry, and this is who?

BROCK: Bob Brock, Hill-Matheson.

SHUMWAY: You mean, *Doctor* Brock? I can't believe you even read / it.

BROCK: *Cell* won't look at it till you've got something with animals. You can teach tumors to dance the mambo, *Cell* won't care if it's still in the dish. Then there's your writing. It's awkward…tentative… no point mincing words, it stinks. Read Whitehead and Russell for style. By the way, who *are* you? I've never heard of you. I only started reading your paper, because I thought it was something else.

(As SHUMWAY *starts to speak)*

BROCK: What I get is you're stitching together D N A snippets from a few genes and slipping them into a cancer cell, where they reprogram it and turn it into this R-cell of yours, is that not correct?

SHUMWAY: I guess you *could* / say…

BROCK: So now instead of always telling itself, "yes, it's time to divide", like a cancer cell does, your R-cell says, "no it's time to stop", is that close enough?

SHUMWAY: Are you / asking…?

BROCK: Well, it's been done.

SHUMWAY: I know.

BROCK: The snippets are smaller, you're jamming in more, but more doesn't make it new. Look, I'm off in five minutes to do a site visit in London. Some important new work on fever. I really can't talk with you now. Hello?

SHUMWAY: Yes?

BROCK: Go on, you were saying?

SHUMWAY: *(Beat)* I'm sorry, what was the question?

BROCK: I see you're at Illinois. Lot of bright people there, I'm sure. Then there's New York. We're six months away from the best immunology department in the world, that's why they call it New York. I'm only going for brilliant here. I can't be bothered with bright. Hello?

SHUMWAY: Hi.

BROCK: Your R-cell doesn't just tell itself no…it goes after any cancer cells around it and wipes them out by telling *them* no…*this* is new. It's not the money, is it?

SHUMWAY: No.

BROCK: Good, that's out of the way. So, what then? No, of course, you like it there. The Midwest, why not? I'm told the wind comes sweeping down the plain. Plus, you work for Ed Paxon. I've known Ed for years, he's exceedingly "bright". There isn't a better program if you're looking for somewhere to die. Let me guess, he wants to make you repeat what you've done in ten different nutrient cultures.

SHUMWAY: *(Slight beat)* Well, he feels in order to / demonstrate…

BROCK: And I'm sure that's a perfectly valid point, but it's also complete bullshit. Ed's the best juicer I know. He can squeeze ten different papers from one piece of work. Life's pretty short, William. Do you want to spend two more years of it still in the dish?

SHUMWAY: I'm sorry…did you just offer me a job?

BROCK: Hill-Matheson, best cancer research institute in the world. New York, best city in the world. Starting in a month.

SHUMWAY: God, that would…any way this could wait / until…?

BROCK: I want you here tomorrow. I'm giving you a month.

SHUMWAY: It's just I'm kind of in / the middle...

BROCK: *(Shouting offstage)* Connie, change my flight and put me through Chicago. I need to stop in Champagne-Urbana.

(BROCK walks towards SHUMWAY, continuing the conversation but now in person)

BROCK: Do you understand the magnitude of what you've already done? People have spent the last thirty years trying to figure out how tumor cells trick us into thinking they're one of us. You're tricking tumor cells into thinking we're one of them. This is one of those moments, when people better cover their heads, because there's a low rumble, old plates are starting to slide apart, and the crust is going to fly. You're taking us down the rabbit hole, and journals like *Cell* don't like getting papers from Illinois that scare the shit out of them.

SHUMWAY: Even if I started shutting things / down tomorrow...

BROCK: *(Pulling a letter from his pocket to show* SHUMWAY*)* This is a requisition for your new animal lab. Do you want me to sign it or not?

SHUMWAY: You mean...back up a second...you're saying I would have my own lab? My own animal lab?

BROCK: I need you, William. This is what I've been chasing for years. And you need me. Say the word, and I'll have you in *Cell* by the spring. I know how to make things happen. I won't let those R-cells just sit there rotting at the bottom of a dish.

SHUMWAY: *(Beat)* I'll need at least two hundred mice, twenty groups of ten...that's to start. And I can be there...what about...all right, make it five weeks... Yes.

(SHUMWAY *shakes* BROCK's *hand and* BROCK *turns to go.*)

SHUMWAY: And make that twenty-five groups of ten!

BROCK: *(Turning back to* SHUMWAY*)* One month! *(He exits.)*

(Lights up on the lab, where SHUMWAY *is working.* BROCK *enters.)*

BROCK: Put down whatever you're doing. Peter Whitcomb's coming up.

SHUMWAY: Now?

BROCK: Exactly what *are* you doing?

SHUMWAY: Waiting.

BROCK: New set of slides?

SHUMWAY: I'm almost ready / to…

BROCK: I think what bothers me most about Peter is his complete self-absorption. He comes to a party, youngest director at Oxford of cell bi…nobody asked to hear his credentials…Nobel at forty-two…fine, say it once. *(Already sitting, as he asks)* Do you mind if I sit? I have a feeling the wine was Almaden. I had to drink quite a lot to kill the taste. Foundation people from Carnegie, Ford…perfect chance to mention the new wing? Not with Peter around. He acts like the only reason people came is to listen to him.

SHUMWAY: I thought the party *is* for him.

BROCK: Well, of course it is, technically. We can't throw a party to get all those people and then say the guest of honor is *us*. Don't give him any specifics. He just wants to snoop around and see if your cell is farther along than his. Hasn't it been five minutes? He said five minutes. *(After several beats)* So…how are you liking New York?

SHUMWAY: Fine.

BROCK: You grew up in Minnesota, I seem to remember. Beautiful country...I'm not interrupting?

SHUMWAY: No. Well, / actually...

BROCK: Good. How about your apartment...plenty of room to prowl around in?

SHUMWAY: Uh-huh.

BROCK: All the appliances work?

SHUMWAY: I guess.

BROCK: That smell of urine...have they gotten it out of the lobby yet? I was appalled to hear.

SHUMWAY: I think so.

BROCK: Any pals yet? Someone to go see a film?

SHUMWAY: Kind of.

BROCK: *(Beat)* William, were you severely beaten as a small boy for talking too much?

SHUMWAY: *(Slight beat)* Oh. Sometimes when I'm working on a new set of slides, I forget to talk. I just try to make myself quiet inside and wait. Sorry.

BROCK: And that somehow...no, I'm interested...how does it help?

SHUMWAY: I guess I've always thought about science as...I don't know, revelation. If I care too much about whether I'm right, it becomes more about pride.

BROCK: Don't tell me you're religious?

SHUMWAY: Well...kind of.

BROCK: No...that's fine...you mean, God, that sort of thing. Have you met the Saudis? Extremely devout people...rearranged their lab so they could do their work facing east. One of my sons, in fact.

SHUMWAY: One of your sons is a Saudi?

BROCK: No, believes in God. Or used to. For years, and I never knew.

SHUMWAY: To me, it's like a jigsaw puzzle. We shuffle pieces around, trying to find which ones look like they go together, when suddenly the entire design / becomes...

BROCK: You know, it's probably just as wise not to talk like this in front of Peter.

SHUMWAY: Think about it. If I hadn't read your paper in June of '93 on mapping peptides...

BROCK: June of '93, I think you're right.

SHUMWAY: ...because if I hadn't, I would never have gone to the meetings in Tucson that year in order to hear you speak.

BROCK: I nearly won the Nobel twice for that work, did you know that?

SHUMWAY: '95 and '99.

BROCK: I got robbed in '99.

SHUMWAY: Your talk completely changed my life...I thought my brain was on fire...

BROCK: Wait a second. You went to Tucson in '93? How old were you then?

SHUMWAY: Fifteen. I thought I'd have to hitchhike, but my mother finally broke down and paid for a bus.

BROCK: *(Beat)* You're very...different, aren't you? *(Slight beat)* Maybe on Sunday, you'll come to the apartment...meet Annie, my wife...second wife, technically. Good, I'll expect you at ten. Why do you keep looking at your watch? It's just time for the regular check, right?

SHUMWAY: *(Slight beat)* Uh-huh.

BROCK: Nothing particular needs saying?

SHUMWAY: No…not necessarily.

BROCK: Is there something you'd *like* to say?

SHUMWAY: Not yet.

BROCK: William…

SHUMWAY: All right. *(Beat)* Okay, here's what I was thinking. Normal cells read each other's signals, which can be "yes" or "no". Cancer cells read only their own signals, which are always "yes, keep dividing"… that's why they're so hard to stop. An R-cell *used* to be a cancer cell and still looks like one…at least that's what *real* cancer cells think, so they let its "no" signals in. The result…"no" from the outside, "yes" from within…the signals start to scramble…then shutdown…meltdown…death. Only it's not that simple, why? *(Slight beat)* One more minute…play.

BROCK: The R-cell always goes after the nearest cancer cell it can find…the R-cell looks and acts just like a cancer cell, so it winds up attacking itself.

SHUMWAY: Exactly. After three or four days, the R-cells wipe themselves out, and the tumors start to grow back. If I could add another gene to the R-cells…one that'll keep them alive long enough…

BROCK: You're not considering bc12, I hope?

SHUMWAY: Actually…I was. If I can isolate the sequence / then…

BROCK: Talk to Peter. He was sure about bc12…then after wasting six months…remind me, I'll dig up his paper.

SHUMWAY: April of '99. He used the wrong sequence. *(Slight beat)* When I read his paper, it made perfect sense. It's just, you know…wrong.

BROCK: So find the right one.

SHUMWAY: I did.

BROCK: That's why the new set of slides? *(Slight beat)* How long before the tumor started to shrink?

SHUMWAY: Fourteen hours...down from twenty.

BROCK: *(Unimpressed)* Fourteen...twenty...what else?

SHUMWAY: I injected the mice nine days ago. Well, eight.

BROCK: How long before they began to relapse?

SHUMWAY: They haven't.

BROCK: *(Beat)* Let me understand. You haven't had a single tumor start to grow back?

SHUMWAY: They're still shrinking...in fact.

BROCK: For eight days?

SHUMWAY: In two more minutes, it could be nine.

BROCK: You do know, it's still much too soon to be sure.

SHUMWAY: I know.

BROCK: *(Unable to restrain his excitement)* Jesus, William, what the hell's wrong with you? You don't think at some point it might've been nice to mention this?

SHUMWAY: I figured you'd say it's much too soon to be sure.

BROCK: Well, it is. So, don't start getting excited, it's premature!

(Lights up on office. ALICE CURITON, a 21-year-old student is seated and talking to BROCK. He is preoccupied, looking for something. his comments are in the spirit of distracted grunts)

CURITON: So, while technically I'm only a junior, I topped out of the undergrad track with my scores.

BROCK: Uh-huh.

CURITON: And now, with the Pauling Fellowship, that pays for space and enough computer time, I can do my own projects...up at Harvard...?

BROCK: Right...near Boston...

CURITON: ...so it's not terribly far-fetched to think you could use me this summer / in your...

BROCK: You know, I'm looking, but I don't see a folder...

CURITON: Actually, I'm sort of pissed. I thought Harvard would have immunology worth doing...with a "C" ...that's Curiton with a "C"...

BROCK: Um.

CURITON: ...or at least down the block at M I T.

BROCK: Down the block, / yes.

CURITON: I guess when eighty percent of the full professors are over fifty, the gears have to slow down / a little...

BROCK: And you sent a cover letter?

CURITON: ...although truthfully, the whole field seems to be getting a little weak in the knees...

BROCK: With a transcript to my attention?

CURITON: ...Yes, B-R-O-C-K, "BROCK". To me, the excitement is elsewhere. Cal Tech...a little crackle and pop at Duke, and, of course, here. Doctor Shumway... his article in *Cell* this month...I thought, "no way he could've shrunk a tumor for two weeks like that"...but after the second read, I had to grab my head to make sure it didn't explode. Then I threw open the window and started shouting how everyone else in tumor research should pack up their things and go home.

(BROCK *steals a glance at his watch.*)

If I was talking too much, you'd let me know, because
I'm a little nervous. You wouldn't just look at your
watch, you'd let me know.

BROCK: *(Slight beat, looking up from his watch)* Uh, yes, of
/ course...

CURITON: Please...all I want is a broken chair in his lab
this summer. Say yes, I really need the challenge.

BROCK: I'm sorry, but I've looked everywhere, and I
have nothing here from you. Now my secretary said I
would see you today?

CURITON: Naturally, I was grateful. Here, I brought
another.

BROCK: And you're sure it was / her?

CURITON: The important thing is I'm here, and we're
meeting.

BROCK: *(Beat)* Miss Curiton, do I look like someone
who can't think of ways to fill his time? You have
no appointment...there was never a transcript...I'm
guessing you called and my secretary...no, please
don't defend yourself. In fact, try not to speak at all.
You're like a thousand poodles barking at once. We
don't take summer students here. We found they were
often in love with themselves for no apparent reason.
They made snide remarks about people over fifty, as
though being young and irritating were somehow an
end in itself. Now I *am* looking at my watch, and I see
it's noon.

CURITON: Then if it's okay, I'd like to take you to lunch.

BROCK: *(Beat)* No need...we understand each other.

CURITON: I have to do this, it's destiny. The science
is perfect and what an incredible story. On one side,
you've got cancer...smart...tough...enthusiastic...
never slows down. On the other, there's a normal, say

a liver cell, divides maybe five times in its entire life.
Which would you bet on? Now take that same cancer,
put it in a room with the R-cells and watch them go…
reading each other…playing off each other…making
the perfect moves. Good and evil mean nothing…it's
the best against the best, every moment electric…and
tragic, because this is war, there's only one winner, and
it's winner takes all. By the end, they know each other
so well, there's a kind of love, and they know they'll
have to destroy the thing they love. It's epic. That's the
kind of science I want to do.

BROCK: *(Beat, then indicating that she should give him her
transcript. a quick glance, he is clearly impressed)* Good,
now we *do* have a folder on you.

(As BROCK *stands,* CURITON *does so as well)*

BROCK: As it happens I'm on my way to Doctor
Shumway's lab. If you want to just say hello…

*(*BROCK *picks up his briefcase and umbrella. They walk.)*

BROCK: So tell me…Alice? Did you have a relative who
died of cancer? A close friend?

CURITON: Excuse me?

BROCK: Something got you interested in cancer
research, that's all I meant.

CURITON: That's what I thought you meant. I'm a
woman, so it's got to be personal. I can't just love
science like you.

BROCK: Miss Curiton, you want something very badly
from me. So if you find me a little patronizing, my
suggestion is…live with it.

*(*BROCK *and* CURITON *enter the lab where* SHUMWAY *is
working.)*

SHUMWAY: Remember what you were saying about the
sequence?

BROCK: Doctor Shumway...Miss, uh...

(CURITON *starts to extend her hand*)

SHUMWAY: *(Pleasant but indifferent)* Hi. *(To* BROCK*)* Isn't today Washington?

BROCK: I thought you might want to hear a little news.

SHUMWAY: Let me show you my idea first. Maybe the tumors start coming back at two / weeks...

BROCK: Did you try cutting that chain out of the sequence?

SHUMWAY: Didn't help.

BROCK: How about increasing / the...?

SHUMWAY: What if instead of increasing the "no signals", I focus on ramping the signal / strength up...?

BROCK: Except you're close to optimal/ strength already.

CURITON: What if you spliced in a gene sequence that varies the signals to five percent "yes"? *(Slight beat)* Sorry.

SHUMWAY: Go on.

CURITON: I think the tumors could be breaking your code.

SHUMWAY: Adding those five will drop the actual "no" signal impact by closer to ten.

CURITON: I know. But if you randomize the five, you could get enough extra scramble to more than wipe out the loss.

SHUMWAY: *(Beat)* Interesting.

CURITON: Really?

SHUMWAY: When we tried it, it didn't work...

CURITON: Oh.

SHUMWAY: …but it's still an interesting thought.

BROCK: *(Beat)* There now…we've met. Unfortunately, Miss Curiton has a train to catch?

CURITON: Right. *(To* SHUMWAY*)* Thank you. *(Shaking his hand. then, shaking* BROCK's *hand)* 'Never overstay your welcome,' that's my motto. *(She exits.)*

BROCK: "If you don't like the way I drive, stay off the sidewalk." *That's* her motto.

SHUMWAY: Then how come you brought her here?

BROCK: I don't know…I was curious?

SHUMWAY: Me too. Why don't I call downstairs and / ask them to…

BROCK: No…let her get back to Boston first. I'll have Connie phone and ask her to come back tomorrow… for an *appointment.* Tuck in your shirt, William. How can you work with your shirt hanging / out?

SHUMWAY: Sorry.

BROCK: The conference planners in Tucson just called. *(Slight beat)* Looks like we're in. They even gave us a Friday slot.

SHUMWAY: Unbelievable.

BROCK: Congratulations on an excellent start.

SHUMWAY: Start?

BROCK: A Saturday slot would be unbelievable. Friday at ten is an excellent start.

SHUMWAY: *(Slight beat)* Aren't you excited?

BROCK: Of course.

SHUMWAY: I mean, how many papers get chosen for Tucson?

BROCK: Very few. *(Slight beat)* But even fewer get picked for a Saturday slot. All I'm saying is don't

forget the difference. Friday at ten is promising. And
promise... *(Referring to* CURITON*)* ...is all you need
when you're her age. But for you, it should never be
enough.

SHUMWAY: No...you're right.

BROCK: *(Suddenly aware he may have hurt* SHUMWAY'*s
feelings. an awkward beat)* You need an umbrella?

SHUMWAY: Why?

BROCK: There's a storm on its way up from Florida.
Take it, I never catch colds.

SHUMWAY: Then why did you bring it?

BROCK: In fact, keep it. I'll just wind up leaving it on
the plane.

SHUMWAY: I'm not upset.

BROCK: It's just an umbrella.

SHUMWAY: I mean, I see your point. Friday isn't
Saturday...you're right.

BROCK: Well, then...enough said.

SHUMWAY: *(Beat, then indicating the umbrella)* I guess I
can always use...

BROCK: I got that in London, you know.

SHUMWAY: Thanks.

BROCK: So, don't lose it. It's a nice umbrella. Well...

*(*BROCK *leaves.* SHUMWAY *admires the umbrella. then,
looking up, he opens it, as though it has started to rain. He is
unaware that* CURITON *has entered the lab, holding a pizza
box. he suddenly sees her)*

CURITON: I decided to take a later train.

SHUMWAY: Miss...

CURITON: Curiton. That's Curiton with a "C". I figured, hey, 12:15, time for lunch… *(Indicating the umbrella)* You in the middle of something?

SHUMWAY: No…they're expecting rain.

CURITON: *(Slight beat)* Yeah, well, I grabbed a few slices down the block. I hope you like pepperoni. *(She sets down the pizza and starts to eat a slice ravenously)*

SHUMWAY: How is it?

CURITON: Delicious. All the pizza in Boston is made by Greeks. Slice?

(SHUMWAY gestures no, as CURITON continues eating.)

SHUMWAY: You might want to think about eating more slowly.

CURITON: Why?

SHUMWAY: You'll burn the roof of your mouth.

CURITON: It's such a waste of time eating slowly. Honest opinion, what do you think of me?

SHUMWAY: I barely know you, Ms Curiton. I was just watching you *eat*.

CURITON: I wish you'd call me Alice. I've got a boyfriend, it's just awkward the other way. *(As she continues eating)* I didn't actually just get back with the pizza, I was waiting for Doctor Brock to leave.

SHUMWAY: I kind of…

CURITON: Plus, I faked my appointment, he could tell. I really don't believe in lying, so I never get to practice, that's why I'm so inept…which should tell you how desperate I am. *(As she hands him a transcript)* In case you want to look while we're talking.

SHUMWAY: Thanks.

CURITON: *(Indicating the transcript)* Anything about it unclear?

SHUMWAY: You're very intense, aren't you?

CURITON: Say I can work with you, and I'll shut up.

SHUMWAY: Part of the problem is you're an undergraduate.

CURITON: Why, because that's what it says on my transcript?

SHUMWAY: Well...yes. It says twenty-one... undergraduate right here.

CURITON: Okay, but that's where the similarity ends. What if I move to New York for the fall...do my senior project with you, while I finish whatever classes...?

SHUMWAY: That's the other problem, I don't have time to teach you.

CURITON: I'm not asking you to teach me.

SHUMWAY: You'd be my student, so wouldn't I kind of have to? I like working alone.

CURITON: All I want is a chance to be around you and watch.

SHUMWAY: Then I wouldn't be working alone.

CURITON: Look, my fellowship travels with me, so you'll be getting me for free...I'll do any job your technicians hate doing, and you just have to go like this when you don't want to talk. It's really not that bad a deal. *(Slight beat)* You're considering it, I can tell.

SHUMWAY: How?

CURITON: You haven't thrown me out.

SHUMWAY: I didn't think you would leave. *(Slight beat)* Your idea before about five percent "yes" signals... how'd you come up with it?

CURITON: It just seemed logical.

SHUMWAY: Adding "yes" to get "no" isn't logical.

CURITON: I did the math.

SHUMWAY: Right, but *before* the math, you had the idea. Where did that come from?

CURITON: I don't know if I can...okay, a couple of days ago I was thinking...then on the train this morning, something else, but that didn't work, so I thought about chicken lo mein for lunch...picked up the idea again...got stuck...thought the smell, we're probably passing through Bridgeport...had another idea...liked the idea...got pissed off...decided on pizza instead... then something different about the feel of the tracks... noticed somebody's hat...thought about "hat" as a metaphor...and suddenly this popped out. *(Slight beat)* Is that okay?

SHUMWAY: *(Beat)* Look, it's only one more year...there are worse things than a degree from Harvard.

CURITON: Nobody there believes in a cure. They treat the word like a relic from some grainy old film about Louis Pasteur. You get tenure by tacking another twenty seconds onto someone's remission. "Being cured" is how children think...like "abracadabra, it's gone".

SHUMWAY: It's only Harvard, so I'm sure you correct them.

CURITON: I used to. Now I just tell them to read your paper.

SHUMWAY: You're twenty-one, Alice, you'll read plenty of other papers.

CURITON: It's too late, yours got inside my brain and rearranged the circuits. Forget trying to kill tumors. You've created a cell that gets them to fall on their swords and die. You've got cells talking other cells into taking a moral position. The whole idea is completely insane and exactly right. Other people might be older and have more experience, but they won't get it like me.

SHUMWAY: *(After a couple of beats)* Do you want to see my favorite toy? *(Indicating a piece of lab equipment)* It's the highest resolution cell counter made. Only places you'll find them are Oxford, Cal Tech and here.

CURITON: How much did it cost?

SHUMWAY: Precisely? A lot. Here's what a level four mouse carcinoma looks like on it.

(SHUMWAY clicks a controller, and a luminescent display appears on an overhead screen. There is a dense cluster of shimmering, yellow discs, with a much smaller number of more diffusely distributed, shimmering blue discs.)

SHUMWAY: Every cell gets a radioactive tag...blue for normal, yellow for tumor and...this is two days after injecting the mouse...

(SHUMWAY clicks the controller, and a modified screen appears, in which some of the yellow discs have been replaced by luminous green ones)

SHUMWAY: ...green for R-cells.

CURITON: Far out.

SHUMWAY: Now at eight days...

(Click, and a new screen, this one with more green and fewer yellow discs)

SHUMWAY: ...12...

(Click, still more green and fewer yellow)

SHUMWAY: ...14...

(Click, the direction has reversed, with yellows replacing blues)

SHUMWAY: ...and the tumor comes roaring back.

CURITON: Any way to break it down by location?

(Click. A grid of vertical and horizontal lines are superimposed over the last display)

CURITON: Nice.

SHUMWAY: Just not specific enough.

(Click. A grid of much finer, closer lines is superimposed over the first)

SHUMWAY: Say I want a closer look at this one.

(SHUMWAY moves a cursor, until it identifies a particular square in the grid. Click. The square is instantly enlarged, so that it completely fills the screen.)

CURITON: Excellent.

SHUMWAY: Now I drop another grid…

(Click. A grid of lines, identical to the first one we saw, is now superimposed on the screen.)

SHUMWAY: …Twenty more times, and I've got data I can actually use. Too much, even for three post-docs and eight technicians. To start, you'll just be learning my procedures from Tom…he's my chief technician. The procedures are really tedious, as is Tom. I don't do things like Harvard, so if you really want to work here, you'll have to start all over with me.

CURITON: Wow.

SHUMWAY: As far as transferring, Columbia's got the best cell biology program in New York.

CURITON: Done.

SHUMWAY: Actually, they like it when people apply. How much time after exams will you need?

CURITON: Figure fifteen, twenty minutes to pack.

SHUMWAY: Then I'll expect you here in June.

CURITON: Doctor Brock said no way till the fall.

SHUMWAY: It's not like there's an actual rule about summer students. He just didn't...you know...want to take *you*. And now...

CURITON: Right, you need to get back to work.

SHUMWAY: Call if you have any questions.

CURITON: *(Beat)* Don't you wish June wasn't so far away?

SHUMWAY: See you then.

(Beat, SHUMWAY *starts working.* CURITON *doesn't leave.)*

SHUMWAY: Yes?

CURITON: I'm just...I feel like someone said, "Here's a dollar. Go buy a perfect day".

(Lights up on SAUL ROTH, *mid-sixties, Chief of Toxicology, and* SHUMWAY *in the waiting room of* BROCK's *office)*

ROTH: Some people eat to live, I live to eat. Even with the ulcer. A glass of tea, maybe an egg in the morning. A light lunch...something dairy...then a sensible dinner. *(Beat)* This is what I'm *supposed* to eat. But am I a good boy? And what's more, I love to nosh. Did you know that man is the only animal who snacks? We've turned eating into a hobby. Sweets, I can live without. You like chocolate, it's yours. But a fresh warm loaf of bread...I believe this is the closest we'll ever get to seeing the face of God. *(Beat)* We haven't been introduced. Saul Roth, Chairman of Toxicology.

SHUMWAY: Of course. William Shumway.

ROTH: Don't be offended, your shirt tail is out.

(As SHUMWAY *tucks it in)*

ROTH: I find when I tuck it *into* the underpants, the elastic keeps it in place. This is just a suggestion. *(Beat)* My appointment was for ten. Then again, what's an hour? My people waited forty years in the desert.

How? We learned to live off our humps. *(Beat)* Here's
something no one knows why. Our taste buds are lined
up in neat little rows.. and yet the nature of human
appetite's a mystery. You're from Minnesota. *(Beat)* I'm
asking.

SHUMWAY: Yes, outside Duluth.

ROTH: Do you know the Epsteins...Abe and Betty?

SHUMWAY: I don't think so.

ROTH: Actually, they live in Wisconsin, but they're
probably the nearest Jews to Duluth.

(BROCK has come out. Both ROTH and SHUMWAY stand.)

BROCK: Saul...forgive me.

ROTH: No, I've been getting acquainted with William.
Still waters run deep.

BROCK: The strangest phone call. A woman from
Newsweek. Anything new on the horizon, that sort
of thing, when all of a sudden she asks if I was aware
some of our people...a Doctor Lazlow for one...
use only *female* sheep, and might there be a political
agenda that her readers should know. I said that was
a fair question and, yes, Doctor Lazlow's sheep *are*
all female, but as Doctor Lazlow is studying cervical
cancer, I wasn't sure how it could be helped. It turns
out I'd heard her wrong. She wasn't from Newsweek
but *Ewe's Week*. They're some radical, feminist, animal
rights group. The thing is, Saul, she's thrown off my
whole morning. You know, instead of trying to find
another time that works for us both...tomorrow's the
Friday talk—why don't you grab me while people are
getting coffee. I can't imagine whatever you need will
take more than a couple...

SHUMWAY: I can come by / later...

BROCK: Don't be silly, Saul's flexible.

SHUMWAY: All I need is / a minute…

BROCK: I'm sure it isn't a problem for Saul.

ROTH: *(Beat)* So, tomorrow. What's a day?

(ROTH exits. SHUMWAY hands pages to BROCK, as they enter the office)

BROCK: I hope these revisions are final, they need to go out today.

SHUMWAY: The schedule for Tucson's been set for a month.

BROCK: When they gave you Friday, your tumors were only shrinking for two weeks…now you're getting five. Peter Whitcomb just applied for a patent…brand new vaccine. I want that Saturday slot.

SHUMWAY: How can Peter…?

BROCK: He says it's in the pipeline.

SHUMWAY: What does *that* mean?

BROCK: When you've got something, you publish. When you've got nothing, you say it's in the pipeline. The press thinks, "Peter Whitcomb, won the Prize at 42…maybe it's something". Drug companies like Pfizer and Merck think it's got to be something, or why all the press? And even nothing, when you water it with fifty million dollars, sometimes a vaccine will grow. *(Indicating the revisions)* Better. *(Handing them back to SHUMWAY)* Get these out today. What did Saul say to you?

SHUMWAY: I have no idea.

BROCK: All those years in the desert? His uncle Milt, who probably doesn't exist?

SHUMWAY: He waited an hour. How come you didn't put off that woman's call?

BROCK: There *was* no woman. He knows that.

SHUMWAY: He does?

BROCK: Of course. Why bother lying to him, if he doesn't know it's a lie?

SHUMWAY: What if he believed you?

BROCK: *Ewe's Week?*

SHUMWAY: *I* thought there was a woman. I was even thinking, 'What an original name for a magazine.'

BROCK: Saul's afraid I may be planning to cut a few of his projects, but he's mistaken, I plan on cutting them all. My problem is, Saul has a lot of friends on the Board, so until my position is stronger…I'm on a leash here like everyone else. If I go to war with Saul, I better be sure I can win.

SHUMWAY: Why does somebody have to win?

BROCK: People are dying from cancer. William. We need fresh ideas, not someone who has to cut short a meeting, when it's time for his nap. You think your lab is big? Well, you need twice as big. That's what Peter has, and the money it takes is embarrassing.

SHUMWAY: Just because Doctor Roth can't still work at the same / level…

BROCK: There are only so many dollars. Do I need to go to the blackboard and draw you a pie? We're in a dogfight, William…This is my job, which I do, so you can afford to be nice. *(Slight beat)* Terrific, now you're upset.

SHUMWAY: No, I…what do you want me to say?

BROCK: How about "thank you"? And be careful…Saul doesn't need to be gunning for you…once the shooting starts, you might still catch a stray bullet standing next to me. So any time he starts in about Uncle Milt, that's when you duck.

(BROCK *turns to address the Board, holding up his hand to quiet discussion*)

BROCK: If I might? I'm beginning to think the Board doesn't quite understand. As of an hour ago, the conference planners in Tucson gave Doctor Shumway a Saturday slot. You're all business people, this is a simple business decision. William Shumway is beachfront property. M I T wants him, Duke wants him...after Tucson, he'll have Europe after him, too. Don't insult him. Give him the money he needs...so the post-docs come here instead of Duke...so he can have the space and equipment he could get in a second at M I T. (*Turning to someone*) Excuse me, I'm still talking! I know you're all busy, this wasn't on the agenda, and there are places you need to be. I don't have time for this either. I've got people waiting to hear your decision from Pfizer and Merck. So until I get an open and binding vote on my budget, nobody leaves this room. I left Yale and came here for one purpose only...to get something done. I still call it the "War Against Cancer". I think of myself as a soldier. I can't compromise on this. If you won't support me... (*Taking an envelope out of his suit pocket*) ...I'll have to submit this as of today.

(BROCK *and* SHUMWAY *in a corridor*)

SHUMWAY: So, there was nothing actually in the envelope?

BROCK: Of course, there was something, it had to look full.

SHUMWAY: What if they opened it and saw you were lying?

BROCK: They already knew I was lying. If the Board thought I was serious, they would have seen me as a hothead.

SHUMWAY: But this way, when they realized you were lying to them…they saw they could trust you? Huh.

(Lights up on BROCK'*s office, as he ushers* ROTH *in)*

BROCK: Saul…come in. Sit. Coffee?

ROTH: Please.

BROCK: With a little milk. You see? I remember.

ROTH: Will you let me say something? Right here, right now, I insist. *(Slight beat)* Bravo. To a successful first year at the helm. Some directors, when they get here, they do a little this, a little that…but not you.

BROCK: There isn't time.

ROTH: You said "the hell with Toxicology. Chemo can go fly a kite. Fuck anyone but me and mine". Which is how it should be…to a point. And the point is this. I heard a rumor about your Doctor Shumway… according to which, you asked the Board to put certain monies at his disposal.

BROCK: I'm not sure why you call it a rumor.

ROTH: My Uncle Milt…a very wealthy man…used to say, "Never get too close to one idea". He was Sephardic…came over in the Diaspora on a camel…

BROCK: Saul…please. This is a copy of my new budget.

ROTH: *(As he reads)* You don't imagine the Board'll approve this / arrogant…?

BROCK: I can assure you they agonized before doing just that ten minutes ago. *(Beat)* I understand your disappointment, Saul. Really, I do. So I wouldn't think of you as disloyal, if you were to consider other offers that might come along.

ROTH: *(Genuinely stunned)* I'm sixty-seven years old. My wife and I are very…comfortable here.

BROCK: I seem to remember you've got a daughter living in Dallas, husband works for Raytheon? Maybe you could find something closer...get to see more of your grandchildren.

ROTH: You know, now that I'm looking more closely, did I say I couldn't live with these? A man can't get to be sixty-seven, he doesn't see flexible as a virtue.

BROCK: The thing is, Saul, it isn't just money for your projects. I'm cutting salaries, too.

ROTH: Well, then...I don't see the problem. My wife, she likes to shop. "Thirty-two years," I've told her, "what can you buy at Bloomingdale's that Macy's hasn't got?" So, exactly how much were you thinking?

BROCK: I really don't want to insult you.

ROTH: Please...insult me.

BROCK: The fact is, I could get three post-docs with the money I'm paying you.

ROTH: Three more years, Bob, I'm seventy. That's when a man is supposed to be old. I'll lie on the beach in Miami...go hear Edie Gorme...in the meantime, all I need is an office with my name on the door. A place to go each morning, I can put on a suit.

BROCK: Saul, I'm really not the bastard you think I am. If you would still like to stay / on...

ROTH: Ask anyone, Bob, I never used the word 'bastard.'

BROCK: ...But about your own office, I don't see how. You know the problems with space here.

ROTH: I guess I didn't make myself clear. The money, I already told you...make me an offer, the answer is yes. But at sixty-seven, without my own office...I shouldn't have to explain / this to...

BROCK: Saul, it isn't just you. I talked with Howard this morning. I'm merging him and Chemo as of / the eighth.

ROTH: All due respect, Bob, Howard's a kid. *(Holding up the list of projects)* These I can swallow. The office, though, I have to insist.

BROCK: No, Saul, you don't get to insist. Not anymore. *(Beat)* So, what do you think?

ROTH: What do I think? Fuck you, is what I think. I've had an office for thirty-three years…since the day I got here from Hopkins.

BROCK: It's in the order of things, Saul…I'm sorry.

ROTH: I've been here through four different directors. At some point, every one of them needed my support…when that day comes for you…

BROCK: You wanted to meet, so we're meeting. I could've just sent you a memo.

ROTH: R-cells come and go. I'll be here to watch the sun burn out.

BROCK: There now…we've met.

(An exclusive men's clothing store. SHUMWAY *is talking from an offstage dressing room.)*

BROCK: How do you like it?

SHUMWAY: It doesn't even look like me.

BROCK: That's the idea. Do you like it?

SHUMWAY: I look great. You don't think it's too expensive?

BROCK: For a Friday, you can pick something off the rack. For a Saturday slot, this is your suit. Hill-Matheson considers it a wise investment.

SHUMWAY: Are they aware it costs over a thousand dollars?

BROCK: Don't worry, the budget provides very clearly for that.

SHUMWAY: Under what?

BROCK: "Miscellaneous." If this isn't "miscellaneous", I don't understand the word.

(SHUMWAY *comes onstage wearing a suit with a white handkerchief, which are identical to* BROCK's)

BROCK: Stand over here.

(SHUMWAY *stands facing downstage with* BROCK *behind him, as though they are facing a mirror.*)

BROCK: Your right shoulder's a little higher than the left.

SHUMWAY: Sorry.

BROCK: One of my sons had the same problem. It's an easy fix.

SHUMWAY: How many...sons?

BROCK: Two. Might've been the other shoulder, I forget.

SHUMWAY: What about a little color for the handkerchief?

BROCK: I don't see it.

SHUMWAY: Are they scientists?

BROCK: No, they're in real estate. Good kids, though... went into business together...their wives are close. We're on good terms. A little distant, that's only natural. With boys, I mean. Bright kids. Not brilliant... bright.

SHUMWAY: *(Slight beat, then shifting his weight)* I had no idea I was asymmetrical.

BROCK: Didn't your father ever buy you a suit?

SHUMWAY: I haven't seen him, since I was five.

BROCK: Ah.

SHUMWAY: Water under the bridge.

BROCK: Understood.

(SHUMWAY *is mouthing words, as he stares at the mirror*)

BROCK: What are you doing?

SHUMWAY: Practicing my talk along with the suit.

BROCK: Why don't you wear it to work? Get used to being the guy in the great looking suit.

(SHUMWAY *senses* BROCK *approach him from behind.*)

BROCK: Just a couple of hairs in back. (*Brushing them off with a tender awkwardness*) There now. Perfect.

(SHUMWAY *enters a lab where* CURITON *is working.*)

CURITON: Great suit.

SHUMWAY: Is it obvious my right shoulder's higher than my left?

CURITON: It's all anyone talks about here.

SHUMWAY: You have the list of which cultures I need you to make, while I'm gone?

CURITON: Yes.

SHUMWAY: The instructions on running the gels?

CURITON: They're on the list.

SHUMWAY: What'll you do if you run out of gel boxes?

CURITON: Look for more behind the fixatives where they always are, which is specified on the list.

SHUMWAY: Where's the list?

CURITON: Right here. (*Pointing to her head*)

SHUMWAY: Alice…

CURITON: And where you posted it on the liquid nitrogen tank and on the tissue culture hood where you also posted it just in case.

SHUMWAY: *(Getting a key out of his pocket)* Doctor Brock thought I should leave the key with one of the post-docs or Tom.

CURITON: How come you didn't?

SHUMWAY: If something went wrong here, they'd all be upset. You're the only one who'd be as upset as me.

CURITON: *(Beat, as he hands her the key)* Listen, a few of the toxicology post-docs were talking…and one of them said he heard you believe in God.

SHUMWAY: *(Slight beat)* And?

CURITON: I defended you. *(Beat)* You're kidding.

SHUMWAY: I never talk about it here.

CURITON: You don't mean literally?

SHUMWAY: This is why.

CURITON: You're a scientist.

SHUMWAY: I don't want to discuss it.

CURITON: Why would you want to believe in something you can't even discuss? This is the same thing I used to get at Saint Agnes.

SHUMWAY: You went to Catholic School?

CURITON: Until they kicked me out.

SHUMWAY: Really? It sounds like a match made in heaven.

CURITON: If they would've just said, "It's okay to be confused. Explaining why babies have to suffer gives us a headache, too." But instead of admitting they don't have the answers, they blamed me for asking the questions. It meant I didn't have faith. *(Slight beat)*

I would've made a terrible Sister Alice...faith always
seemed like just rolling over to me. Although the funny
thing is, I wanted them to be right. I always wanted to
give myself over completely to one huge, spectacular
idea, and now I have...it just isn't God. *(Slight beat)*
I used to envy the girls who had faith. Their brains
may have been assembled from a kit, but they had
pleasant dispositions...they weren't always angry and
disappointed like me.

SHUMWAY: Why were you disappointed?

CURITON: I don't know...that there were so many
beautiful, terrifying questions, and nobody else seemed
to care. When I was little, I couldn't fall sleep at night,
so I asked my parents to explain the dark. They said,
"Here's a nightlight, you'll be fine", but I knew the
dark was still there.

SHUMWAY: My mother takes cream in her coffee. I used
to ask her to drizzle it slowly, because I loved watching
the swirls. One morning I noticed the swirls in her
second cup were completely different from the first...
but after she stirred, the color looked exactly the same.
I was terrified, so I asked her if the world was like that
color...an illusion of order hiding a true condition of
chaos.

CURITON: What did she say?

SHUMWAY: "God works in mysterious ways...but
don't worry...you'll understand everything as soon as
you're dead." *(Slight beat)* I think God...whatever we
call God...never reveals itself to us directly...only in
the traces it leaves behind. We have to listen for it in a
trail of echoes. I think God is the order of things...but
the world is so full, it's hard to find that order. It gets
buried in the sheer amount...the chaos and riddles...
the coffee swirls. Look at the R-cell. 'The enemy of my

enemy is my friend.' The logic of a possible cure, and it's buried in a paradox.

CURITON: It sounds kind of Buddhist. I guess Buddhist is okay. *(Slight beat)* Do you ever worry you'll get all the way to the bottom of those coffee swirls, and there *won't* be an order, just more swirls?

SHUMWAY: No...that's what makes it faith.

CURITON: So where is the bottom...how do you get there? I don't even know where to look.

SHUMWAY: You can't find it by looking. You have to listen. If you're quiet and alert enough, maybe you'll hear.

CURITON: I'm too impatient. Teach me to listen like that.

SHUMWAY: There's no way to teach it. I picked you, because you already can. *(Slight beat)* Your idea on the train from Boston that time...that wasn't something you figured out...you started listening, and then you heard.

CURITON: *(Beat)* Do you want to have sex?

SHUMWAY: I thought you have a boyfriend.

CURITON: I've decided I like you better. *(After several beats)* This is embarrassing.

SHUMWAY: No, it's a nice...thought.

CURITON: *(Slight beat)* You're not gay...on top of being religious?

SHUMWAY: You're my student, it wouldn't be right.

CURITON: I know two post-docs who are practically engaged to their lab chiefs.

SHUMWAY: Post-docs aren't students.

CURITON: So you can't have sex with me, but you can with someone you don't even trust with your key?

(She walks over and seems about to kiss him) That makes
sense. *(She adjusts the knot on his tie)* Knock 'em dead in
Tucson.

(As CURITON *is about to leave:)*

SHUMWAY: Alice...you won't be a student forever. Rain
check?

(Lights up on BROCK, *talking into his cell phone)*

BROCK: No, I want Doctor Shumway in the penthouse
suite, right where you booked him over a month...
excuse me, am I still talking? You screwed up, and
that's okay, now live with it. As a scientist, I pride
myself on being dispassionate. But as director of this
institution, I'll have our attorneys sue your hotel till it
bleeds. *(Beat)* Good, then. And make sure the quiche
and those little meatballs are hot.

(Lights up in the lab. BROCK *enters.)*

BROCK: Tell me again, slowly this time.

SHUMWAY: I was checking weights on the new group of
mice when I noticed several...their glands are starting
to swell.

BROCK: You finish checking all your other mice?

SHUMWAY: Three times.

BROCK: Any swelling with them?

SHUMWAY: All the other groups seem fine. It's just the
new one.

BROCK: This is why I had to "stop whatever I'm
doing"? Last month, when the glands in that other
group started to swell...

SHUMWAY: I know.

BROCK: Were those animals beginning to relapse, or
was it a simple infection like I said?

SHUMWAY: And I'm sure it's a simple infection again. ninety-nine percent sure.

BROCK: Good. Can I go now? I've still got a million things to do before tomorrow.

SHUMWAY: That's the problem, Tucson's tomorrow. There's no time to section the tissue.

BROCK: So, you'll section it when you get back. Now go home and get some sleep.

SHUMWAY: Is that what you think I should say?

BROCK: About what?

SHUMWAY: In Tucson. When I mention the group, say there wasn't time, I'll section it when I get back.

BROCK: Why even mention it?

SHUMWAY: *(Slight beat)* You mean…I guess I'm not sure what you / mean.

BROCK: One group means nothing.

SHUMWAY: Right, so why not / mention it?

BROCK: Why do you think final drafts had to be in a month ago? Something always comes up at the last minute, everyone knows that.

SHUMWAY: Uh-huh. So, if everyone knows that…I guess I'm still not / clear…

BROCK: Why, do you think there's something to worry about?

SHUMWAY: No. I'm sure as soon as I section / the tissue…

BROCK: You'll be addressing reporters…idiots with an M B A. It would take a week to explain the magnitude of what you've been doing. You'll have forty-five minutes, tops. Out of which, you'll have their undivided attention for ten. By the time they've had a

couple of cocktails, they'll remember maybe two things
you said, and trust me, this will be one.

SHUMWAY: I'm sure if I can be matter-of- / fact...

BROCK: Do you want to listen, or did you wake up
today knowing more than me?! *(Beat)* You can't expect
people like that to understand science. If an animal
dies, all they know is it's dead. People are bringing
their checkbooks tomorrow. And you want to stand
up and give them what people with money love the
most...a perfect excuse not to spend it.

SHUMWAY: *(Beat)* So then...you're saying as long as I
deal with it right after Tucson...

BROCK: Obviously, if it turns out there really was a
problem, you let people know right away.

SHUMWAY: I guess bringing it up before I've had any
chance to investigate...it's not like we're trying to
publish. *(Slight beat)* The funny thing is I already had
one foot out the door. If I hadn't decided to check one
more time...

BROCK: Listen, I told the driver to pick me up first. That
way you'll get a little more sleep.

SHUMWAY: Thanks. You're not angry?

BROCK: About what?

SHUMWAY: It just seemed the tone of your voice...

BROCK: "The tone of my voice"...honestly, William.
(Slight beat) I can't believe we're still up. Excited?

SHUMWAY: You bet.

(A spotlight on SHUMWAY, *who turns to address the
audience in Tucson)*

SHUMWAY:...And in conclusion...I truly believe that
some day we'll look back on cancer the way we look at

cholera today…as the curious suffering of a primitive people.

(Applause. Lights on ROTH *and* SHUMWAY, *as the sound fades,* ROTH *still clapping and pointing his finger playfully at* SHUMWAY*)*

ROTH: I knew him when, I knew him when…Very nice, very professional. In case your ears have been burning, a couple of rows behind me, I overheard someone, "This young man, if there wasn't already the Prize, they would have to call Sweden and make one." You probably don't know, I brought down a little something myself they want me to read. Should you happen to find yourself with a few extra minutes…

SHUMWAY: If there's any way I can / come…

ROTH: …The last I heard, they moved me to Monday, right after something very important on pus. You try the Jacuzzi?

SHUMWAY: Actually, there's…one in my room.

ROTH: I'll probably skip it. Looking across at a bunch of naked scientists…the idea alone, I want to throw up. It would be quite an honor…winning the Prize at your age. Younger than Watson…almost as young as Heisenberg.

SHUMWAY: Younger than Heisenberg…actually. Listen, I should probably…there's a little reception upstairs… of course, you're welcome, / if you'd like to come…

ROTH: You're very thoughtful, but I mostly came over…I was waiting at the front desk before…? You don't want to hear the toilet they gave me…and the man saw me wearing Hill-Matheson… *(Indicating his I D tag, with name and affiliation)* …said a woman from New York sent a fax, did I know where Doctor Shumway…?

(Holding up an open envelope, with a folded fax inside, he hands it to SHUMWAY, *who starts to read)*

ROTH: Everything okay?

SHUMWAY: Yes.

ROTH: Good. You know, for such a young man, I admire your poise.

SHUMWAY: Thanks. I was a lot more nervous than I looked.

ROTH: I mean right now. If it were me, I'd be on the phone... *(Indicating the fax)* ...asking what she means by "something the matter with two of your groups".

SHUMWAY: *(Slight beat)* Anyway, I really need to...

ROTH: Please, go mingle. Maybe when we're back in New York, you'll come see my office, meet my new roommate...we'll sit down and talk.

*(*SHUMWAY *in the lab. The phone rings. As he answers, lights come up on* BROCK, *who is calling from a pay phone in the Milan airport.)*

SHUMWAY: Hello?

BROCK: Listen, my cell phone died, can you hear me all right?

SHUMWAY: Where are you?

BROCK: The airport in Milan.

SHUMWAY: I've been trying to reach you.

BROCK: Arnie Pollock just tracked me down. You remember meeting him in Tucson last week... had that God awful toupee?

SHUMWAY: *The New England Journal*...sure.

BROCK: Apparently, they're going to print in a week, and an article just kicked out. Do you have a clean draft of your paper from Tucson?

SHUMWAY: Yes.

BROCK: Get it out to him today…someone is faxing you details.

SHUMWAY: *The Journal* wants to run it?

BROCK: What do you think we've been talking about? There's no time to put it through regular peer review, but if he gets it today, he can fast track it and have it in galleys by Friday.

SHUMWAY: Friday?

BROCK: William, Pollock's calling it the most exciting work he's seen on tumor research in more than ten years.

SHUMWAY: I thought we said Tucson was different from trying to publish.

BROCK: Right, if there turned out to be a problem. *(Beat)* William, you have to talk louder. This airport seems to be filled with infants that haven't been fed.

SHUMWAY: Another group is involved.

BROCK: I know…you showed me the girl's fax.

SHUMWAY: I mean, another one since then.

BROCK: Why's that surprising? If the infection from the first group spread to / the second… ?

SHUMWAY: It wasn't an infection. The mice were starting to relapse.

BROCK: *(A couples of beats)* Anything else different about those groups?

SHUMWAY: No. They're all from the latest batch that got shipped / but…

BROCK: You're sure?

SHUMWAY: I don't know why that would / matter.

BROCK: How many times do mice get infected, before they're even / shipped?

SHUMWAY: It wasn't / an infection.

BROCK: I'm just saying as an example. Anyway, this has nothing to do with *The Journal*.

SHUMWAY: Nothing / to…?

BROCK: You'll only be publishing the groups before Tucson.

SHUMWAY: Right, but wouldn't we still want to…? We'll only be losing a couple of months.

BROCK: It doesn't work like that. *The Journal*'s locked up for more than a year. Get him the draft today, will you? This sort of break never happens. Look, my plane is boarding… *(He seems about to hang up.)*

SHUMWAY: I really think we should talk / about this…

BROCK: Fine. What if I try to reach you sometime / tomorrow?

SHUMWAY: I need more time! *(After several beats)* I'm sure it's / just…

BROCK: Okay, William…maybe you'd better tell me right now. Is the pressure getting too much for you?

SHUMWAY: What do you / mean?

BROCK: All the attention…everything moving so fast…

SHUMWAY: That's got nothing to do / with…

BROCK: Your project's the only thing on my calendar. I've never given anything this kind of focus, but I can't keep making the R-cells my life, if you're not completely sure.

SHUMWAY: I just told you I'm sure.

BROCK: And I heard that, but are you *sure*? Because the people on top of money mountain want better than kind of pretty sure. Tucson got you off the farm, made you credible, but these people have spent the last thirty years and billions of dollars on a cure that was always around the corner, but the cows never came home, so when they listen to a paper in Tucson, they're hearing *every* paper that nearly cost them their jobs...this time they want to be sure.

SHUMWAY: How?

BROCK: A letter in writing from God, but he said no... *The Journal's* the closest thing.

SHUMWAY: *(Beat)* And Doctor Pollock is clear, he'll only be getting results before Tucson?

BROCK: Just the groups you presented there.

SHUMWAY: So, all I'll be saying is ten groups of mice were injected with the human equivalent of a level four carcinoma...

BROCK: Right. Can I tell him yes?

SHUMWAY: ...the tumors continued to shrink for five weeks before stabilizing...I don't see how I'd be overstating...

BROCK: It's practically word for word from your talk.

SHUMWAY: He needs it by the end of the day?

BROCK: Don't worry about typos, his editors need the work.

SHUMWAY: I just want to make sure it's clear when I sectioned the latest group.

BROCK: As long as he gets it by the end of the day.

SHUMWAY: So he really liked my talk?

BROCK: 'The most exciting work in over ten years'... Arnie Pollock.

SHUMWAY: Hurry, you'll miss your plane.

BROCK: Are you near a cup?

SHUMWAY: A cup?

BROCK: Coffee cup…or just grab a beaker. You got it?

SHUMWAY: Yes.

BROCK: Now raise it.

SHUMWAY: Okay.

BROCK: Because I'm about to propose a toast. Is it in the air?

SHUMWAY: Yes.

BROCK: *(Holding the phone in one hand, he raises the other)* To Sweden.

END OF ACT ONE

ACT TWO

(SHUMWAY *in lab, dictating notes. Although each entry is spoken as if it just happened, we hear pages being printed continuously as he speaks)*

SHUMWAY: September 17. In the mice that have relapsed, something odd. R-cells are declining in number, but no cell debris or any other sign they died. September 22. As expected, cancer cells are increasing as the R-cells decline, but by a strange coincidence, both events are happening at almost the same rate. *(He begins collecting the pages and putting them into a manila envelope.)* September 29. No coincidence. The rates aren't close, they're identical. Can only mean these R-cells aren't dying…they're turning back into cancer cells. October 3. Initial attempt to keep these cells from turning back has proven unsuccessful. May need to consider destroying the renegade R-cells. Will require disabling the bc12, which has been keeping the R-cells alive.

October 10. Initial attempts to disable the bc12 have proven unsuccessful, as it appears to have deeply embedded itself in the renegade R-cell's code. *(He has begun walking to* BROCK's *office with the envelope)* It is becoming harder to ignore the real possibility… maybe just a new set of eyes…

(BROCK's *office.* SHUMWAY *is carrying the manila envelope)*

BROCK: *(Interrupting)* Try to picture…every single meeting…some of those people I go back twenty years…first chance to talk in God knows, but it was "Hi, how's Annie", and that was it for the small talk. Everything else was *your* work, *your* paper in *The Journal*, and where do they send the check? This whole trip…everything had a shine…here, it's Madeira, I picked it up at the duty-free.

SHUMWAY: No, / thanks.

BROCK: *(As he pours the Madeira anyway)* Not to say "I told you," but as soon as your paper ran in *The Journal* this month, Stan Griffin…runs the animal program at Yerkes? …said give him six weeks, he'll free up a primate lab, and if that doesn't sound premature enough… Do I look younger to you? First words out of Annie's mouth, I dropped five years while I was gone. Oh, and listen, there may be a situation in Brussels over the next couple of months and if that works out…

SHUMWAY: See, while you were / gone…

BROCK: I'm sorry, I thought I was talking. *(Slight beat)* No, go ahead. I'm not really supposed to even be mentioning Brussels…I'm just so…please, tell me everything…start from the…oh, but first, I know you'll get a kick out of…Sherman Fraser…sits on the Nobel selection committee…said guess whose name in cell / biology…

SHUMWAY: Speaking of premature…

BROCK: Exactly right, and so was guessing Hodgkin or Pauling would win it until / they won.

SHUMWAY: I don't even know Sherman Fraser, why are we talking about the Prize?

BROCK: I just thought you'd get a kick / out of hearing…

SHUMWAY: No, you're always…all that matters to me is the science. These other / things…

BROCK: I know it's the science. Don't you think I'd be doing the science myself if I had any choice?

SHUMWAY: What do you mean, / "had any"…?

BROCK: I turned fifty, William. I can even tell you the moment I suddenly knew the science was gone. I went for months without a single, original thought. I began having, and I don't mean headaches…I felt like my brain was so starved, it was starting to feed on itself. And then the…ugh…those sweaty three in the morning…I had a few that scared the shit out of me.

SHUMWAY: What happened?

BROCK: What usually happens to scientists, after they can't have an original thought? I was made chairman of my department. I spent the next few years slowly dying at Yale, then Hill-Matheson called…I figured bigger's got to be better, but it was just a bigger graveyard, until one day I opened the mail, and there was a paper written across the street from a pig farm in Illinois. And I had a reason to get out of bed again. *(Slight beat)* Anyway, I'm sorry…I had no idea my saying the Prize upset you. It's the last time you'll hear me mention the word. I really just wanted you to know how everywhere I went…not that I needed anyone to tell me, but it made me…and I'm sure it's just human nature, but I felt…proud. I felt proud of you.

SHUMWAY: *(Beat)* Christ.

BROCK: You're right…enough said. The floor is all yours.

SHUMWAY: You just got back.

BROCK: Exactly…and now you're going to tell me everything I missed.

SHUMWAY: It can wait.

BROCK: It doesn't have to, I'm back! Any more problems since those three groups?

SHUMWAY: *(Slight beat)* Just a few technical problems... nothing I can't solve.

BROCK: So, it was only that one batch of mice?

SHUMWAY: Isn't that what you assumed?

BROCK: Yes. *(Slight beat)* Is anything wrong?

SHUMWAY: Such as?

BROCK: You just seem...ever since you got / here.

SHUMWAY: Well, I'm not. Just tired.

BROCK: Tell you what. Give me an hour to go through my mail, there's a new Thai place...this one's / even better...

SHUMWAY: Thanks...if there was any way I could.

BROCK: *(Slight beat)* Maybe Sunday. At least promise you'll knock off early.

SHUMWAY: In which case, I should probably...
(Indicating that he is ready to leave)

BROCK: So there's nothing I need to know?

SHUMWAY: Not about that.

BROCK: Not about what?

SHUMWAY: *(Slight beat)* Whatever we've been talking about.

(As SHUMWAY turns to go, BROCK indicates the envelope.)

BROCK: William, isn't that for me?

SHUMWAY: It's nothing.

BROCK: Then why did you bring it?

SHUMWAY: Don't worry. The sky didn't fall, just because you were gone.

BROCK: *(Beat)* Do me a favor, William? Get some sleep.

(SHUMWAY, still holding envelope, and ROTH in corridor)

ROTH: There you are. Everyone I talk to, it's the same story. "He never calls, he never writes…"

SHUMWAY: I've been incredibly busy.

ROTH: Enough with the mice, it isn't healthy. Why don't you give yourself an hour tomorrow, you'll come to the Friday talk.

SHUMWAY: As soon as I have something to say…

ROTH: Nobody goes there to *say* anything, we just *talk*. Fridays are when we all come together…talk a little science…enjoy a little nosh…and remind ourselves the enemy is cancer, not other departments. You're a nice, young man, I mean that…very respectful, and I know you're close with Bob. He's almost, what, like a father, and I commend you, but fathers are difficult…busy… they find us wanting, and then they go. So if there's ever something you'd like to discuss…

SHUMWAY: I have no idea what you're talking about.

ROTH: *(Slight beat)* Don't apologize, half the time I don't know either.

(SHUMWAY joins CURITON in the lab.)

CURITON: So right around five weeks…?

SHUMWAY: A couple of days faster or slower, depending on the group, but that's when every animal's starting to relapse. *(Indicating the manilla folder)* This is everything.

CURITON: So if the R-cells are turning back into cancer cells…okay, who am I? Cute little squirrel, under the fur, I'm really a rat? No…more like a hired gun…

SHUMWAY: What are you doing?

CURITON: Trying to think like an R-cell. "Hired gun... soldier of fortune"...you need them, so you use them, but you're always careful, you know they can turn.

SHUMWAY: *(Slight beat. Becoming interested)* And when they do turn?

CURITON: You go in, wipe them out, and replace them with new recruits...other R-cells that *haven't* turned.

SHUMWAY: And when *those* new recruits start to turn...? *(He is thinking along with her, not asking.)*

CURITON: You wipe them out, too.

SHUMWAY: So you just keep repeating...not bad, except the bc12 won't let me. The same gene I spliced into the R-cells to keep them alive, now it won't let them die. It's protecting the R-cells from *me.*

CURITON: What about another gene to disable it?

SHUMWAY: There isn't one.

CURITON: p55.

SHUMWAY: How would you get it into the cell?

CURITON: Hide it in a virus...let the virus slip in...why you're looking at me like I'm crazy?

SHUMWAY: Do you know how long a chain p55 is?

CURITON: Not the whole chain...just the small, active sequence.

SHUMWAY: No one's ever been able to find it.

CURITON: So find it, then you'll be famous for that, too.

SHUMWAY: It might not even be small.

CURITON: On bc12, it was.

SHUMWAY: Finding an active sequence can take years.

CURITON: On bc12, it took you a couple of weeks.

SHUMWAY: I had Peter Whitcomb's paper, I didn't have to make the same mistakes / that...

CURITON: It's just an idea! Instead of telling me how stupid / it is...

SHUMWAY: It's a *great* idea. I'm just mad we didn't talk sooner, we could have been working on it now. What are you doing tonight?

CURITON: I did sort of promise my boyfriend...

SHUMWAY: *(He hands her a large notebook)* You're going to need to start learning this.

CURITON: *(As she flips pages)* It's the entire protocol.

SHUMWAY: Yes.

CURITON: I've never seen anyone here with more than the pages they're working on.

SHUMWAY: If you're going to start running groups...

CURITON: You'll let me help?

SHUMWAY: No, Alice, this was your idea...I'll be helping *you*. Tomorrow I'll tell Tom to take you off any projects...you know, when the post-docs realize I've given you the protocol, it could / get...

CURITON: They barely speak to me. They never ask me what I'm working on, and I don't bring it up.

SHUMWAY: *(Slight beat)* Okay, then. Maybe I'll just do a few things, so tomorrow morning...

CURITON: *(Readying herself to join him)* Why don't I start running the gels?

SHUMWAY: *(Slight beat)* Don't you need to call your boyfriend?

CURITON: Sure. About what?

(BROCK in SHUMWAY's lab. BROCK holds a piece of paper)

BROCK: Peter Whitcomb copied me on this.

SHUMWAY: It was just a misunderstanding.

BROCK: You weren't taken aback by his tone?

SHUMWAY: For some reason, Peter thinks I'm obliged to send him results from every group the second I finish / running it.

BROCK: That isn't quite what he's / saying.

SHUMWAY: You know the time / it takes...

BROCK: You haven't published anything since *The Journal*, and that's fine, but in the meantime, I know it's a pain in the ass, but as the knighted director of cell biology at Oxford, yes he's entitled, and yes you're obliged.

SHUMWAY: I've been busy. New idea. *(Slight beat)* Fine.

BROCK: Don't forget, N I H needs those plans for the new sheep lab. Until they see an actual / plan...

SHUMWAY: Anyone else besides Peter?

BROCK: What?

SHUMWAY: Who's been asking about my results.

BROCK: Yes. Let's see...everyone? Arnie Pollock...it was his decision to fast track your paper by skipping peer review...

SHUMWAY: What do you tell them?

BROCK: "He's from Minnesota, they've got their own way of doing things there." Remember I mentioned Brussels a couple of months ago? While I've been gone, I made another side trip there to meet some people from Pfizer. They're close to coming in with us.

SHUMWAY: How close?

BROCK: Another few months...if everything goes smoothly. They're willing to frontload enough development money to bury Peter's vaccine. Which is not to say we don't like Peter, we do...we're happy to hear Christmas with his sister in Cardiff went well, but mostly, we hate him, just like he hates us. That's why whenever we deal with Peter, we're always *polite*. So as soon as we're finished talking, you'll give him a call.

SHUMWAY: And say what?

BROCK: Jesus, William, you're a grownup, make something up. *(Slight beat)* I expect you to handle these things, because you're my guy. Don't ever forget that, William. You're my guy. *(Beat)* Now if we're finished discussing Peter, I'd like to move on to that student of yours.

SHUMWAY: I've already spoken to her.

BROCK: I must've had five messages from Omar Qahtami, while I was gone.

SHUMWAY: Did he tell you she apologized? And truthfully, I don't think it's fair to say she was *blasting* her / music...

BROCK: But for her to / tell him...

SHUMWAY: I'm not making excuses...I know she doesn't always think...

BROCK: Just incredible. What is she, twenty-one?

SHUMWAY: I'm sure being so young is part of it.

BROCK: I mean, it's incredible she's managed to live long enough to *be* twenty-one. "Doesn't *think*?" She nearly caused an international incident.

SHUMWAY: I don't think she realized how insulting...

BROCK: She didn't realize "don't be a dick" is insulting?

SHUMWAY: I mean how coming from a young woman...given their patriarchal / society...

BROCK: If she had to insult a Saudi, why couldn't she pick one who doesn't know enough English to realize how offensive she was. Qahtami's brother is married to the Crown Prince's niece. If they stop sending us graduate students, that's two million dollars a year. I want you to transfer her to another lab.

SHUMWAY: What are you talking about?

BROCK: It's obvious you can't control her…you're too nice. She needs someone like Stalin.

SHUMWAY: She's my student. She moved here from Boston to work with me.

BROCK: Fine, and as her supervisor, you now feel she's ready to broaden / her…

SHUMWAY: I disagree.

BROCK: I wasn't asking if you agree.

SHUMWAY: That new idea…we've been working on it together.

BROCK: So get Whasisname, that post-doc from Princeton or…it's either that, or she's gone.

SHUMWAY: No, I need her.

BROCK: She's a student! If Quatami's gripe was with you, I'd've told him, "Sorry, William's my guy. You don't like it, go call your king". But to take the side of a student…you find talking with her helps, take her to lunch, but I want her out of your lab.

SHUMWAY: She needs to learn the procedures. Once we're ready to start running groups / she'll…

BROCK: You haven't given her a copy of the protocol?

SHUMWAY: How else can she learn?

BROCK: William…Pfizer's biggest concern is security. How do you think they'd react if they knew your protocol's in the hands of some twenty-year-old who can't shut her mouth?

SHUMWAY: If she's going to run her own groups…

BROCK: And if you've been listening at all, you know she never will.

SHUMWAY: I've been teaching her for weeks, she can almost run them now.

BROCK: *(Beat)* Are you having sex with this girl?

SHUMWAY: No.

BROCK: That's too bad. At least it might explain what's happened to your brain. *(Beat)* All right...the last thing I want is to put more pressure on you. You want to tell me about this new idea?

SHUMWAY: No. I mean, not until there's something to tell.

BROCK: Just move her for a month. As soon as Qahtami's had a chance to cool off...

SHUMWAY: I already know what her position will be.

BROCK: I'm sorry, her *position*? Her only position is to smile, as she's dragging her things down the hall, because I am this close to picking up the phone and calling Ted Burke at Columbia, and believe me with that kind of note in her file, she can forget about grad school, forget about *science*...

SHUMWAY: All right! *(Beat)* I'll talk to her.

(CURITON and SHUMWAY in the lab)

CURITON: And did the topic of Doctor Qahtami's disgustingly overbearing attitude towards women ever come up?

SHUMWAY: Doctor Brock is serious.

CURITON: How does transferring me make any sense? The only person I get along with is *you*. Just tell him we have too much work. Maybe he doesn't really get what we're working on. All that "friend of a friend of an enemy" ...exactly how did you describe it?

SHUMWAY: *(Slight beat)* I don't remember "exactly".

CURITON: Well, he obviously didn't get it. Or else he'd be saying, "Fuck Qahtami, and you two, back to work".

SHUMWAY: I told him the same thing I'd tell anyone else.

CURITON: Okay, so what do you tell *them*? *(Slight beat)* Say another lab calls…"we hear you haven't been running groups, is there something new"…what do you tell them?

SHUMWAY: Since when did how I talk become such / a problem?

CURITON: I just think if Doctor Brock isn't getting it, maybe I should give it a try.

SHUMWAY: *(Slight beat)* You think he's going to meet with you?

CURITON: He has to. Page one in the student handbook, "Please feel free to bring me your problems".

SHUMWAY: No, Alice.

CURITON: I don't see how / it could…

SHUMWAY: No.

CURITON: Why not?

SHUMWAY: This has nothing to do with you.

CURITON: What do you / mean?

SHUMWAY: Whatever I say to Doctor / Brock…

CURITON: I'm just trying to / help…

SHUMWAY: I said no!

CURITON: *(A couple of beats)* Sorry.

SHUMWAY: What do know you about Doctor Jorgenson?

CURITON: The pancreatic dysplasia guy…had a stroke last year?

SHUMWAY: He's still on the adjunct list…I could assign you to him.

CURITON: This the guy who lost oxygen…kept confusing the physical therapist with his wife?

SHUMWAY: The point is he doesn't come in. He won't mind if you keep working with me…or even remember you're supposed to be working with him. And Quatami won't care what you're doing as long as he doesn't see you *here*.

CURITON: If I'm still working with you, he *will* see me here.

SHUMWAY: Not if we only work at night. *(Beat)* Are you all right with this?

CURITON: *(Slight beat)* What the hell…I'm mostly up at night.

(BROCK's office. SHUMWAY carrying three notebooks, one of which is fairly thick)

BROCK: Sorry about the rush. Connie just got me on the one morning flight to Brussels. *(Referring to the notebooks)* Those the latest groups I asked for?

SHUMWAY: This is everything. We need to talk.

BROCK: Pfizer just wants the latest stuff to see what you're working on now.

SHUMWAY: This one's the raw data. This one's all my diary notes.

BROCK: Fine, I'll look them over on the / plane.

SHUMWAY: *(Thrusting one notebook at BROCK)* You need to look at them now.

BROCK: *(Feeling how light the "raw data" folder is)* I thought you said this is everything. *(He opens the*

notebook, flips through pages) July...August...where's all
the stuff since Tucson?

SHUMWAY: These two are October.

BROCK: I see, but then nothing in November...
December...

SHUMWAY: Remember I mentioned a new idea...?

BROCK: Now I'm in January...

SHUMWAY: ...so instead of running more groups...

BROCK: Right, there wouldn't be as many, but this is
March.

SHUMWAY: When you go though all my diary / notes...

BROCK: I've got a plane to catch, William, boil it down.

SHUMWAY: If I'd known you were taking the early /
flight...

BROCK: It's a simple question, where are the other
groups?!

SHUMWAY: Okay, just...these are the ten groups I ran
before Tucson. This column / here...

BROCK: I can see all that. Are you saying ...?

SHUMWAY: Notice wherever new cancer cells start
appearing, the R-cells always decline...I just assumed
they were dying, but they aren't, they're turning back
into cancer cells. So what I tried...

(Beat)

BROCK: It's been six months, William! Didn't you
realize the longer you went / without...?

SHUMWAY: Yes! I knew every day was another day
since *The Journal*, but it was also another day to fix the
problem...and I knew I could, I just needed a little
more time...then Peter Whitcomb or Arnie Pollock
would ask me to send them something...I'd say there's

nothing to send, and they'd say, "Fine, just send us whatever you've got", so that's what I sent them... nothing. I / never...

BROCK: William...

SHUMWAY: ...Let me finish! ...I never lied or made up...these aren't excuses...and then one day you said, "Pfizer...Brussels"...I couldn't just let you go to Brussels, so finally there was a deadline. Now.

BROCK: Listen, William...people are going to ask me, so I need to know...when is the first time you realized this was a serious problem?

SHUMWAY: Seventeen days after Tucson...I can show you exactly / when in my notes...

BROCK: Jesus.

SHUMWAY: ...You were back from a trip...I had a manila envelope...you wanted to see it, remember?

BROCK: Yes, you wouldn't let me.

SHUMWAY: All my results were in that envelope, but I couldn't show you...not the way you were acting.

BROCK: How was I acting?

SHUMWAY: Excited...

BROCK: I *was* excited, I thought I had a reason to be. Something, though...I felt like grabbing the envelope out of your hands.

SHUMWAY: I know, why didn't you?

BROCK: Why didn't I "what"?

SHUMWAY: *(Slight beat)* Maybe you should cancel the trip.

BROCK: Every one of Pfizer's chief marketing directors from around the world is flying in for these meetings. I've been assuring them for months that everything's fine, moving / ahead...

SHUMWAY: Again, I'm not making excuses, but that isn't how I remember / the...

BROCK: Right, a few technical problems, nothing you couldn't solve.

SHUMWAY: I never actually told you I solved them, and you never asked.

BROCK: I never had any reason to ask.

SHUMWAY: Didn't you? *(Slight beat)* Look, I know I'm responsible, I kept / avoiding...

BROCK: No, that was the second comment you've / made.

SHUMWAY: I'm sorry, but if you're going to tell me I said things were moving ahead...I was so careful never to actually tell you / I'm making progress...

BROCK: "Actually"'s got nothing to do with this, William, I thought it was true, and so did everyone else, because that's what I told them, so what do I tell them now? Those people are made out of money and ice.

SHUMWAY: I knew publishing was a mistake.

BROCK: No, realizing you had a serious problem, then sitting on it and ducking questions for the next six months...why the hell did you wait so long?

SHUMWAY: I don't know. I didn't want to upset you... what does it matter, they're all stupid reasons? Maybe I thought you didn't want to know or if I could fix it / before...

BROCK: See, there it is again...maybe I didn't want to know. If you had any doubts, all you ever had to do was sit down and / ask me...

SHUMWAY: When?! You were never here. I'd get a call from some airport, everyone around you screaming in Spanish...

(As BROCK *glances at his watch)*

SHUMWAY: You always seemed to be saying my project's so important, it's all right...not to lie, you never said *lie*...the line seemed pretty clear, but then it stopped being so clear, and then we stopped talking about it at all.

BROCK: Interesting...now can we focus? *(As he reads a page in the diary notes)* It's just unfortunate, William... not everyone is this precise. I've been on site visits, most of the entries, there wasn't even a date.

SHUMWAY: *(Slight beat)* Just so I don't get the wrong impression again. You're not asking me to alter the dates?

BROCK: All I meant... *(Slight beat)* Jesus, William, we were this close!

(As BROCK *opens his cell phone:)*

SHUMWAY: What are you doing?

BROCK: Calling Pfizer. / They...

SHUMWAY: Don't. *(Slight beat)* That new idea, the one... You remember Alice? *(Slight beat)* My /...

BROCK: Curiton ...with the mouth. You haven't told her about *this*, have you?

SHUMWAY: Pretty much.

BROCK: Unbelievable. I thought you reassigned her.

SHUMWAY: Yes. No, I didn't. The idea was hers. Please...look. *(Handing* BROCK *a small notebook with data)* The biggest problem was bc12, finding a way to disable it. No one's ever done it, and we couldn't figure out how. Now we have.

BROCK: *(Reading, impressed)* Just these two animals?

SHUMWAY: So far. We had to make sure it works.

BROCK: How soon before you could start running groups?

SHUMWAY: A month.

BROCK: You don't think you're / being...?

SHUMWAY: A month is conservative, no.

BROCK: *(Slight beat)* Exactly how does Miss Curiton understand all of this?

SHUMWAY: All she knows is I ran into a technical problem, and she's getting a chance to help. She doesn't realize she's the only person I told...or that I'm having *this* conversation with you...and I promise she won't. So whatever happens next is up to you. *(Indicating the three notebooks)* The last six months are right here, and I take full responsibility for them. Whatever I *thought* you were saying...you never actually said it. *(He picks up the three notebooks and offers them to BROCK)* Now you know everything. So if you go to Brussels and leave anything out, then you'll be responsible too. *(Slight beat)* One more month. I need that month. I've been living like this for so many months, I can take one more. You don't have to. You can make it end right now...call the Board...say you just learned some shocking information...it's all up to you.

(Beat, then BROCK opens his phone and dials)

BROCK: Connie, tell the driver I'm on my way down.

SHUMWAY: What if Pfizer insists on seeing the latest stuff?

BROCK: Fuck Pfizer. We'll go to Merck.

(SHUMWAY and ROTH)

ROTH: William, do you mind if I...which way are you walking? *(Slight beat)* So, the thing I was curious...what would be a good situation for you?

SHUMWAY: "Good situation"?

ROTH: In the sense of not so much good but acceptable.

SHUMWAY: "Acceptable"?

ROTH: Say, in the sense of any situation that's better than the one you're in now.

SHUMWAY: Do you have something specific in mind?

ROTH: William, please. Even if I had any idea what you meant, that sounds like a whole different conversation from the one I'm trying to have.

SHUMWAY: Are we finished?

ROTH: When we're finished, you'll be the first person I tell, that's a promise. *(Beat)* When you look at me, what do you see? Some people see a person who's a little old…whose name is never mentioned along with the Prize…and for these crimes, he was sentenced to die. So, how is it Saul Roth is still Chairman Roth on the same committees and plays in the same Friday night card game with certain important men on the Board… if at the same time, he's already dead? It's a real conundrum. How I resolve it is those men are friends, and they in concert with other friends would also like to have you as a friend.

SHUMWAY: And all I'd have to do is give up a different friend?

ROTH: Can he offer you protection? Only a true friend can promise you that. It's a funny thing…sometimes the person we always thought was our enemy turns out to be our only friend. *(Gently)* There's a lot of weather moving in. I could be…a harbor.

SHUMWAY: This is so easy for you, isn't it?

ROTH: Truthfully, William, no. *(Beat)* Do you mind if I speak my actual thoughts? *(Slight beat)* Whether or not you believe, this gives me no pleasure. You've always struck me as a bright young man with an honest wish to do good. I'm guessing to you, most of what people worry about is nonsense. If a bunch of grown men want to act like two-year-olds fighting over a marble in a room full of toys, that's got nothing to do with you, except trust me, William, it does. Nonsense can grab hold of you...then wrap itself tighter and tighter, until one day you can't get out...not without help, but as much as they want, it's too late, no one can give you that help, you waited too long to ask them, you should have asked for it *now*. *(Beat. Then he takes a card out of his pocket and offers it to* SHUMWAY*)* Sunday...3 A M...doesn't matter...if this is something you'd like to pursue, try that first number, I check it / at least...

SHUMWAY: No, this...I don't know what this is supposed to...I shouldn't even be / listening...

ROTH: William...

SHUMWAY: No! Just leave me / alone!

ROTH: Or you'll do what, call the principal?! I don't know if they taught you in Minnesota that pain doesn't hurt, but this is your life...don't be a putz.

SHUMWAY: *(Beat)* I need to go.

(Several beats, as ROTH *continues to hold out the card.* SHUMWAY *finally takes it.)*

*(*CURITON *and* SHUMWAY *in the lab)*

CURITON: *(Beat)* Look, I'm disappointed, too...but there's a lot to be encouraged...it's the first group we've run, and *most* of our assumptions turned out to be correct. *(Slight beat)* I think we're only talking about a series of small adjustments now, not a change in the model. *(Showing him a list)* If we try them, say, in this order...

SHUMWAY: We can't combine any?

CURITON: How?

SHUMWAY: This could take six weeks.

CURITON: About that, / so?

SHUMWAY: I'm in trouble.

CURITON: It's one group.

SHUMWAY: If you had any idea…

CURITON: People will understand…first group today, new procedure…

SHUMWAY: They won't understand, I never told them.

CURITON: Not that it was "today", but they know it's the first group…

SHUMWAY: I don't mean which day or what group…I never told them *any* / of this.

CURITON: The point is they know it's a new idea, and / whenever…

SHUMWAY: Please be quiet!! *(Beat)* You once asked me what I told colleagues…when they asked me to describe it…remember?

CURITON: Yes, you / said…

SHUMWAY: I *didn't* describe it…to anyone.

CURITON: I don't…what do you…?

SHUMWAY: When they called, I promised to get back… and of course, I *intended* to …as soon as…but then…

CURITON: As soon as what?

SHUMWAY: I knew we were this close… so, if I…

CURITON: Close to *what*? I don't understand / what you're…

SHUMWAY: …if I could just hold everyone off / a little…

CURITON: What are you talking about? I'm not following any of / this.

SHUMWAY: I know, but the thing is...the thing is, Alice...you are.

CURITON: *(Beat)* So when labs would call ...?

SHUMWAY: Yes. Labs ...N I H...I never told anyone.

CURITON: No one?

SHUMWAY: Except you.

CURITON: Why didn't you just call and tell them, "Look, I'm having a problem ...as soon as I have more information..."?

SHUMWAY: I don't know.

CURITON: What do you mean you don't know?

SHUMWAY: No one stopped me from calling. I don't *know*. I didn't want to make it sound more serious than it / actually...

CURITON: You don't think this / is serious?

SHUMWAY: It is *now*...but before Tucson, when it still seemed like a simple / infection...

CURITON: What do you mean, "before Tucson"?

SHUMWAY: The point is I wanted to tell someone, but I didn't, and the longer I went / without...

CURITON: So why are you telling *me*?!

SHUMWAY: There's no one else! You're the only one who might listen instead of...you *know* me.

CURITON: Right, I know how hard, how much pressure... and I care about you. So what?! What does any of that have to do with *this*? They could fire you. That's what they'll do, won't they?

SHUMWAY: Not if I fix it in time.

CURITON: "Time"? Nobody's going to give you *time*. Once they realize…

SHUMWAY: Yes, *once* they realize. Let me see that list for a / second.

CURITON: What good will / the list…?

SHUMWAY: *(Referring to the list)* You just said it…six more weeks…

CURITON: I can't keep this a secret. You know that.

SHUMWAY: Look, I'm sorry…I know it isn't fair to put you in this / kind of position.

CURITON: No, it isn't. Why do I have to be the one / who …?

SHUMWAY: What about this? Tomorrow I'll have Tom put you on a different project…you'll be completely removed from / any…

CURITON: And then what…pretend you never told me? I have to report this, you know that, and the moment I do, everything will be over. *You* did this…why did you have to make *me* responsible? You had no right.

SHUMWAY: What if you…? *(Referring to her list)* Just give me enough time to run one more group after I've made these adjustments…

CURITON: It's over.

SHUMWAY: …If there isn't any improvement, you have my / word…

CURITON: No! I have to stop this…it's obvious you can't.

SHUMWAY: All I'm asking is six more / weeks…

CURITON: Don't you realize what you've done?! If you had told people there was a problem, someone else might've solved it a month ago…and we'd be one month closer to a cure. Did you ever think about how

many people will die in that month? *(Beat)* Why didn't
you talk to me sooner? I've been right here. I would
never have hurt you. *(Beat)* You were everything.

(BROCK *and* CURITON *in his office*)

BROCK: I appreciate your coming directly to me.

CURITON: I thought if I tell you, and you tell the
Board…you know how to talk to those people…I just
don't want to see him get hurt by this any more…well,
than he has to.

BROCK: I'm surprised you're not angry.

CURITON: I was. But I think he may have been trying
to protect me. From myself. If he had told me this
six months ago, maybe the idea of holding back
information to buy some time… *(Beat)* Is he all right?
He hasn't been in the last two days.

BROCK: I asked him not to, until you and I could talk.

CURITON: Do you think there's a chance he could get to
stay on? I really thought we were on the verge…

BROCK: Maybe you could help clarify…after you called,
I poked around a little myself, and this paperwork
turned up. It looks like he transferred you to a Doctor
Jorgenson?

CURITON: Yes…after that misunderstanding.

BROCK: "Misunder"…could you be more specific?

CURITON: I think you were out of the country. Doctor
Qahtami became involved?

BROCK: What's that got to do with Jorgenson?

CURITON: You asked Doctor Shumway to transfer me
out of his lab. That's why we started working at night.

BROCK: I said you should work at night?

CURITON: No…that was Doctor Shumway's idea. You
may have been away at the time.

BROCK: And I suppose I'll have to answer for leaving Doctor Shumway to flounder so much on his own. I still don't see why Doctor Jorgenson? He can't remember to brush his teeth.

CURITON: I never actually met with him.

BROCK: Then / why…?

CURITON: Is this really what we need to discuss?

BROCK: We won't know, until we've discussed it.

CURITON: *(Slight beat)* Doctor Shumway picked him, because he never comes in. I know how that sounds, but he only did it to protect the work, and I'm concerned if you focus on that kind of trivial deception / people…

BROCK: I was going to ask what your own signature is doing on the transfer agreement. *(Slight beat)* And on this document from Columbia…do you see right here?

CURITON: Obviously, I went along, I just don't see…do you really think it matters?

BROCK: That's something you might want to ask an attorney.

CURITON: *(Slight beat)* I'm not sure what we're doing right now.

BROCK: You're the only other person who knew about his problem all those months.

CURITON: Not that he was concealing it.

BROCK: You didn't wonder why he never sent out status reports?

CURITON: How would I know what he was sending?

BROCK: You worked side by side at the bench with him for months.

CURITON: As a student.

BROCK: On your idea. Is that why? Twenty-one years old and your hero, devoting / himself...

CURITON: The only reason I'm reporting / this...

BROCK: Please don't insult my intelligence by saying you're only after the truth. We both know you better. The first words you ever said to me were a lie. You stood right there and swore we had an appointment, which my secretary, in a signed deposition...

CURITON: Don't threaten me.

BROCK: I haven't even started.

CURITON: I was his student, he reported to *you*. Your name went on his papers. You ran around hawking his results.

BROCK: And regrettably, as you've pointed out, that "hawking" kept me from being here. Meanwhile, you spent every night with him...which I personally don't believe ever led to the sort of intimacy our guidelines clearly prohibit, but others may be more skeptical, especially after Doctor Shumway's attorney is finished with you.

CURITON: He has a lawyer?

BROCK: Ms Curiton, you're accusing him of fraud. You'd better start to think about getting one yourself.

CURITON: I only came here... *(Beat)* I just wanted to help.

BROCK: *(Slight beat)* Understand, I have nothing against you. You're an extremely bright, determined young woman. I also find you an irritating, pompous know-it-all, but if memory serves, that's what everyone thought of me. I'm only trying to show you the pitfalls of your plan.

CURITON: I don't have a plan.

BROCK: You aren't planning to take this to someone at Columbia...maybe even the Board, if I advise you to drop it.

CURITON: I guess I'd / have to.

BROCK: If you're really sincere about wanting to help, let me suggest how. First, I need to tell you...about a month ago I became aware of Doctor Shumway's problem.

CURITON: *(Beat)* Well, fuck me for not having guessed.

BROCK: I've only known a month...not very long when you stand it alongside a whole career, but this is whining, let's talk about you. That first group wasn't all we'd been hoping, but your idea on what the next steps...Doctor Shumway thought possibly six weeks...I think you see where this is going.

CURITON: I hope not.

BROCK: I honestly believe that a second group makes more sense than Columbia or the Board. You'll just destroy Doctor Shumway...the R-cells along with him...and you'll never know if all you would have needed was six more weeks. *(Slight beat)* Ms Curiton, you're twenty-one years old. How many people will ever have this kind of chance to alter the landscape of science and improve human life?

CURITON: You don't just want me to shut up, I'm supposed to keep working with him?

BROCK: It's murky, I know. Just remember, we're all trying to cure the same disease. As long as I keep a hard, tight focus on that, the murk always seems to burn off.

CURITON: And if I can't do that?

BROCK: Then we go down that other road. It's your move, Ms Curiton. If you'd...

(Sound of intercom. BROCK *picks up the phone)*

BROCK: Connie, we're just finishing... *(Beat)* He's here now? *(Beat)* Tell him I'll call as soon as...you know what? Just send him in.

(SHUMWAY *enters)*

SHUMWAY: I'm sorry for just showing / up like this.

BROCK: Ms Curiton and I are done talking anyway... she was about to make her decision.

SHUMWAY: *(To* CURITON*)* I'm glad you're still here. I'd like to hear / what you...

CURITON: No, I don't want to be part of any / discussion...

SHUMWAY: *(Sharply)* Please. *(Slight beat)* I've been going through my diary notes, and you know what I realized? They're good. Clear...honest...I thought "these are something a responsible scientist would write, not me...but I *did* write them, they're mine. If I just attach them to a letter describing the problem... when it began...what I tried to fix it...then emailed everything to *The Journal*...Peter Whitcomb...the Board..."

BROCK: William...

SHUMWAY: *(To* BROCK*)* ...not mentioning *you*... *(Back to* CURITON*)* ...then someone else might read the notes and figure out how to fix it...all those people won't have to die because of me.

BROCK: What / people?

SHUMWAY: *(To* BROCK*)* I can't fix it...not in time. If everyone's going to find out what I did anyway, I want them to hear it from me.

CURITON: He's right. What do you have to lose?

BROCK: You mean, besides *everything*? In case you haven't noticed, we're not all living in heaven yet. Around here, the lions don't sleep with the lambs.

CURITON: You need to let him / decide!

BROCK: No! And don't imagine he's going to because of you. Doctor Shumway just needs time to think. Tomorrow he'll forget all about this, and nobody's going to care what some annoying, loud-mouthed / little...

SHUMWAY: I already sent the email.

CURITON: *(Beat. To* BROCK*)* Your move.

(A park. BROCK *and* SHUMWAY*)*

BROCK: Mendel lied, did you know that? Copernicus, too, but their ideas were right. And now those men are legends. The men who accused them...who even remembers their names? Granted, Mendel never sent an e-mail.

SHUMWAY: *(Beat)* Yesterday the doorbell rang, and there was a basket of fruit...from the Saudis...along with a note. "Don't despair. In the great march of time, the individual means nothing." *(Beat)* All they've got against *you* is Alice's word.

BROCK: What do you think the Board's trying to tell me, when they appoint a committee to investigate and put Saul Roth in charge? No, I'm out...but there may still be a chance for you. Another two hours, we're supposed to go before the Committee...now suddenly Saul wants to meet in a park? Hill-Matheson has become unclean. To be allowed back into the world, it needs a cleansing slaughter...something to send a shudder throughout the land, and killing some misguided cherub from Minnesota won't do it. The Board needs to nail a head on the castle door, and mine's the right size, but all they can prove is I didn't

go over your homework with you. That's enough to
fire me, but it won't make them clean. So I think Saul
wants to make a deal...you get off, if I say I knew what
you were doing, and I approved.

SHUMWAY: He tried getting me to blame you...said if I
changed my mind, here's his card, I should give him a
call.

BROCK: How come you never told me?

SHUMWAY: In case I decided to call.

BROCK: *(Beat)* You think I don't know you, William? A
team of wild horses, you wouldn't have called. *(Beat)*
I'm going to take him up on the deal.

SHUMWAY: No, this was / my...

BROCK: You want to keep shouting over me, or do I get
to talk? You let me handle Saul. All you need to do is
start with how sorry...in fact, if there's any way...no,
forget that...if you cry, you cry...

ROTH: *There* you are. *(As he enters from offstage)* Nice
park...very restful. Although, frankly, I'm not too big
on the outdoors. Give me a room...any room. It never
rains in a room. So...do we want to take care of this
now, or would we prefer to drown in a sea of lawyers?

BROCK: Now is fine. William?

SHUMWAY: *(Slight beat)* About seven months ago, I
ran into a serious problem with my research. It soon
became clear just how serious...but I concealed that
until a week ago. I'm ready to tell the Committee
everything at two. *(Slight beat)* For what it's worth, I'm
sorry.

BROCK: I gather you've already suggested to William
how he might show remorse by describing any involve
/ ment I might...

Roth: Naturally, the conversation to which you're referring I have only the barest recollection, but perhaps I was thinking the time for remorse was then.

Brock: Come on, Saul, you've got kids his age...he's a good kid, just look at him.

Roth: The time to look at him was weeks ago. Today all I want to know is did he violate the sacred code of science / by concealing...?

Brock: Can we cut the shit right now, Saul? I know he's dealing from a weak hand, so if you'll agree to show him compassion, I'm willing to tell the Committee at two / that...

Roth: Bob, if you want to write a note on William's behalf, that's fine, but two o'clock's just for him.

Brock: Am I not being clear? I'm ready to give them my statement.

Roth: You want to write how he squeezes milk for orphans out of his tit, the Committee will read your note...but nobody's asked you for a statement.

Brock: Then why did you want me here?

Roth: As a witness...so William can't renege later on what he just said.

Brock: *(Beat)* I just assumed as the senior person...

Roth: We've reviewed all the evidence. The only possible conclusion is William acted alone.

Brock: *(Slight beat)* So, as far as what the girl...?

Roth: She claims you knew, but nobody found her credible...seems to be a problem there with older men. Bob, you and I have had our differences, but the Board is convinced you're the best man to steer us through this difficult time.

Brock: I just assumed...huh.

ROTH: *(Beat)* Why, what kind of statement? *(Slight beat)* You're not suggesting...? Because if that girl was telling...it might change things for William completely. Given how young, we might just be looking at some sort of leave...a little counseling... Is that what happened, Bob? Tell me you knew what William was doing, and I'm sure the Committee will be moved to reach out to him. Of course, if you didn't know, the only place William will ever get to do science again is in his garage. This is awkward, isn't it? *(Beat)* So, what should I say when I get back?

BROCK: Tell them I blame myself for what happened. My job was to be there for him, and I failed.

ROTH: As a department chief, I know exactly the feeling, and I commend you for bringing it up. But that wasn't exactly my question.

(Aware that SHUMWAY *is staring at him:)*

BROCK: I was away so much of the time. That's not an excuse...there *is* no excuse.

ROTH: I feel we're still talking around it. Did you know he was hiding results?

BROCK: Hill-Matheson was becoming a fat, overbred country club when I got here. I brought it back to what it once was. Look at the post-docs that went to Yale this year, and who do you see? The ones who couldn't make the final cut here. So if you want to know can I sleep at night, the answer is yes.

ROTH: Good, finally an answer. Only what was the question? I'm pretty sure it wasn't *my* question. The Board found out William was hiding results a week ago. What about *you*?

BROCK: Why are you doing this, Saul?

ROTH: He's waiting. You like to play God, this is your chance. Tell William if he's been written into the Book of Life.

BROCK: There has to be some other / way...

ROTH: Not at me...look at William. He wants you to look at him while you speak. When is the first time you knew?!

BROCK: *(Beat)* I got an e-mail from Doctor Shumway... there was an attachment...his diary notes.

ROTH: So, a week ago, like the rest of us. Before that, you had no suspicion?

BROCK: *(Beat)* No.

ROTH: William...is there anything you'd like to add?

SHUMWAY: *(Several beats)* No.

ROTH: Take whatever time, just to be sure. There's nothing else you can recollect?

SHUMWAY: No.

ROTH: Nothing else you might, say, between now and two?

SHUMWAY: Doctor Brock didn't know. I'm responsible. That's my statement. *(He takes card out of his pocket and hands it to* ROTH.*)* I keep forgetting to return this. If the Committee asks, I'll swear I acted alone.

ROTH: Doesn't really matter, does it? Even if you wanted to say it was Bob, the Committee would've seen it as, what...a desperate man as he teeters on a ledge. *(Staring at* BROCK*)* Everyone knows how it is with a desperate man...when he starts to fall, he just grabs at whatever he can.

BROCK: *(Finally understanding)* You didn't need a witness, did you? Nothing either of us said would've

mattered. The Board already made up its mind. I stay,
he has to go...this was just to humiliate me.

ROTH: *(Slight beat, then to* SHUMWAY*)* I don't know how
to make you believe this is never what I wished for
you. Maybe there's something else I could have said
you would have come to me sooner...I don't know.
Some people believe our entire lives were written
before we were even born, so maybe nothing either of
us did could have changed the way this has to end. *(He
exits)*

BROCK: *(After several beats)* Did you know I was the
youngest post-doc at Princeton, when Arthur Kornberg
picked me out of everyone and took me under his
wing? Had me out to his place on the beach...I played
cards with him and his wife...shared a room with his
son, Thomas. Kornberg was a family man, but I could
never do both. I lost a marriage...two grown sons who
despise me. My whole life has been science. Thirty-
eight years, William...it would've been as though I
never lived at all.

SHUMWAY: *(Beat)* Just tell me...did you know? Back
when it started, I mean...did you? Everything I
did...I thought we *agreed*...the R-cells were the most
important...no, the *only* thing...so no matter what it
took...you didn't have to come out and say it...I knew
you wanted it too. *(Beat)* Did I just imagine that? I
thought we did it together. Was it always just me?

BROCK: And if I say you didn't just imagine it, will /
that...?

SHUMWAY: No, it won't help if it isn't true. I don't
understand the past six months any more right now
than while I was living them. I need to understand
what happened. All I'm asking is a place to start. I can
use whatever you tell me...as long as it's true. If the

truth is you had no idea, and I imagined it all…at least it's a place to start.

BROCK: *(Beat)* That time I asked you to give me the envelope, and you wouldn't…I felt like grabbing… *(Beat)* Of course, I didn't…no one just grabs. But when you took it with you… *(Beat)* I think when you took it with you, I felt…relieved.

SHUMWAY: *(Slight beat)* Thank you.

BROCK: That's as close as I know how to get to it. I can't give you anything more.

SHUMWAY: I know. *(Beat)* Okay…I can work with that.

BROCK: *(Beat, looking out)* I used to love this pond. When my kids were young, we'd drive down from New Haven on a Sunday, buy a loaf of bread…best times we ever had were feeding those ducks. Then the animal rights crowd decided the ducks were chasing the bread to the bottom and getting strangled in the weeds. Seems no matter what you try to do, it's wrong.

(BROCK and SHUMWAY exit as ROTH enters addressing assembled reporters.)

ROTH: Concerning Doctor Shumway, the evidence is clear that we are dealing with a limited man who tried to lie his way into greatness. Rest assured that from this day forth, he will walk through the corridors of science…as a pariah. Concerning Doctor Brock, we find…no hint of impropriety. He did nothing more than allow a younger, less principled colleague to play upon the goodness of his heart. Our sympathies go out to him and his family. That is our statement.

(CURITON enters. ROTH turns to start scene with her)

CURITON: I've asked N I H to investigate your findings.

ROTH: You'll never meet a nicer group of people, but they're lazy. So if you want to grab their attention, you'd better have proof.

CURITON: I told them everything Doctor Brock said when I met with him.

ROTH: And they said?

CURITON: "Try us again, if you have any proof."

ROTH: As my Uncle Milt used to say...

CURITON: Save it. So then I called a reporter at the *Times*. I said, "Look, every person who reads your paper has cancer, or it's killing someone they love, and if they thought fraud, then a cover-up...the only problem is I don't really have any proof,' and she said 'that's something we can talk about more over lunch,' so tomorrow at one, we're having lunch.

ROTH: Miss Curiton...when you look at me, what do you see?

CURITON: A jaded, corrupt...

ROTH: That was a rhetorical question! *(Slight beat)* You want to call me a name, you're probably right, but on two things, my family and science, don't ever question me about ethical. This situation goes way beyond what a jerk everyone in the world is but you. *(Beat)* Bob Brock's name is on over five hundred papers that have come out of his labs. Now suppose we catch him at fraud. Is this the first time he's done it? How many of those papers aren't worth the paper they're printed on? What about the thousands more that are based upon his? Just how real are any of the things we think we know? Once you start asking these questions, there's nowhere to turn for comfort. So forgive the Board for deciding...it's better not to start.

CURITON: But it's okay to make Doctor Shumway a "pariah"? That isn't fair.

ROTH: My grandson talks about fair, and he's five. Content yourself, as I do, Bob Brock'll be gone by the fall. This way the noise'll die down…better for him… better for us…better for science.

CURITON: Doctor Shumway came up with a brilliant new way to think about cancer, and you told everyone it's shit. How is that better for science? I don't know what else to do except meet this woman for lunch.

(As CURITON *turns to leave:)*

ROTH: We're still talking, please. *(Beat)* So what I'm thinking…nobody wants to go anywhere near those R-cells, but if a student wanted…as a kind of intellectual exercise…

CURITON: Is this what I / think…?

ROTH: You are, I assume, intending to go to graduate school. Do you expect a great many letters of recommendation, or have you pinned all your hopes on Doctor Quatami. What if you continued at Columbia…a student's application can sometimes be… expedited…you could continue to pop over here…?

CURITON: Yes, it *is* what I thought…a bribe.

ROTH: It's an offer. It's only a bribe if you don't deserve it. *(Slight beat)* The Committee reviewed all the notes from Doctor Shumway's latest group. To be truthful, I'm not convinced the whole idea of R-cells will ever amount to much…but then I'm an old man, it's not the science I know. Still, I could appreciate the beauty of an intricate, rigorous protocol like his. I could also see from his notes whenever an adjustment was needed, the person with the most creative idea usually wasn't Doctor Shumway…it was you.

CURITON: What makes you think I'd be willing to stay here?

ROTH: You're twenty-one years old. I'm offering you space...equipment...animals...and no interference. This may be the only chance you'll ever have to work on the R-cells again. And you don't even have to say thanks.

CURITON: *(Slight beat)* You don't understand...

ROTH: Perhaps I do. And if this love...may I call it that...if somehow you could get people to see it wasn't his fault alone, would that get him into heaven? Would it give him back his seat at the bench, so you could work together again?

CURITON: *(After several beats)* What sort of funding would there be?

ROTH: Certain monies can be made available. As far as specifically, should I inquire? *(Beat)* This reporter...you said tomorrow at one? Why don't I call the lawyers, we can do signatures at ten.

CURITON: How do I know "once the noise dies down", you won't find a way to get rid of me, too?

ROTH: How do I know there's really a reporter? *(Slight beat)* In thirty-three years at Hill-Matheson, I've never gone back on a handshake.

CURITON: It doesn't strike you as wrong...I get to work on the R-cells after I turned him in?

ROTH: You're also the only one who can save them. It's a real conundrum. As my Uncle Milt used to say, "Only she who causes the wound can heal it".

CURITON: How?

ROTH: By proving you're as smart as you think. And when Sweden calls to give you the Prize, dedicate it to him. *(Slight beat)* That's if you really think you're that smart. Otherwise, turn down my offer and have

a nice lunch. *(Beat. He extends his hand to shake hers.)*
Tomorrow at ten?

(CURITON looks at ROTH's hand, hesitates, considering)

(Black out)

END OF PLAY